Sweet Truths

Divine Treats
Surpassing Chocolate

Cynthia Dianne Guy
and
Judi Davis Dean

Publishing Designs, Inc.
P.O. Box 3241
Huntsville, Alabama 35810

Editor: Peggy Coulter

Cover images: istockphoto®

Page images: VectorStock®

Cover and interior design by Crosslin Creative

Printed in the United States of America

Publisher's Cataloging-in-Publication

Guy, Cynthia Dianne, and Dean, Judi Davis
Sweet Truths / Cynthia Dianne Guy and Judi Davis Dean
Nine chapters. Activities and Thought Questions.
1. Chocolate—Christian Living. 2. Transformation. 3. Christianity.
I. Guy, Cynthia Dianne; Dean, Judi Davis. II. Title
ISBN 978-0-929540-86-3
248.8

To Our Beloved Sister

Donna Avinelle Davis Florich
1955–1992

When speaking of chocolate, we often hear the terms "bitter" and "sweet." Those words come to mind as we make this dedication. This time, however, they are combined: "bittersweet."

We dedicate this book to our dear sister Donna who lost her battle with leukemia on August 11, 1992. That was a bittersweet event. Bitterness usually tries to overcome us when we give up someone we love, but how sweet it is to know that Donna was ready to meet the Lord and that He took her from all her pain and suffering.

Donna inspired us. She could make or create anything needed. She made us laugh. Through her illness, she was positive to the end. Her life was full!

As you reflect on the unpleasant aspects of personal events, we pray that you will use our thoughts to see the sweetness of living for God, that you may live a full life in Christ as Donna did.

—Cynthia and Judi

Contents

The Davis Girls, 1963
Left to right: Donna, Judi,
and Cindy

The Davis Family, 1978
Left to right: Donna, Doris, Wilton,
Cindy, and Judi on the floor

Introduction

Only one word is needed to describe a busy woman: *stressed*. But there's a cure. *Stressed* spelled backwards is desserts! This book is designed to help you understand life, just as you understand your sweet tooth. It will whet your appetite for much more than a taste of dessert!

Chocolate is a great stress-reliever. It's our favorite delicious escape. So when we really need a fix, what do we do? Go to the kitchen and make fudge! We think Mom is the reason chocolate gives us comfort. When she was in a terrific mood, or wanted to get in a good mood, she took us into the kitchen and made fudge. That great smell still lifts our spirits.

The scientific name of the seeds from which chocolate is made is *Theobroma cacao*, "food of the gods." One of the links on Hershey's website explains that chocolate contains naturally occurring substances that affect our mood. You will be glad to know that chocolate is an antidote for PMS, depression, and food cravings. We know about food cravings because when we eat chocolate, hunger vanishes!

Chocolate contains an alkaloid closely related to caffeine. But Hershey says that most likely we crave chocolate because we enjoy its taste or we associate it with special occasions. Most of us have a passion for chocolate because we associate it with fond childhood memories.

We warn you—chocolate can put the pounds on. Perhaps a chocolate lover created women's fitness centers. When Erma Bombeck was preparing to sign up for an exercise class, she was told to wear loose clothing. "Are you kidding?" she asked. "If I had any loose clothing I wouldn't need to take the class!"

The delicious theme of this book relates our spiritual walk to chocolate. The familiar quote, "Life is like a box of chocolates," is a

springboard for these lessons. We will examine eight ways that life is like chocolate. How delicious!

Let's begin this sweet "food for thought."

CYNTHIA'S VIEW

What did you learn from studying and researching this topic?

I was most impressed with the fact that life, like chocolate, is brief; so we should enjoy it, share it with others, and pass the recipe for happy, spiritually healthy living on to our children and grandchildren.

How do you feel about *Sweet Truths*?

This book is the first joint effort Judi and I have made. Its theme came from our ladies' days presentations, "Life Is Like a Box of Chocolates." Our early memories of childhood include Mother's delicious fudge, so we tried to incorporate and compare life's struggles, relationships, and joys with some unique characteristics of our favorite treat—chocolate. Our goal is to stir the hearts of readers to a renewed appreciation of God's Word and to illustrate its blessings in the daily lives of Christians.

How will the reader benefit from *Sweet Truths*?

❀ *By confronting the brevity of life.* The reader is reminded and inspired to stop and smell the roses! The book discourages procrastination and encourages living life to the fullest—pulling out the fine china and wearing that favorite perfume often!

❀ *By reexamining her incessant influence on others.* Every woman's influence is great on those with whom she is in contact, especially on her children and grandchildren. *Sweet Truths* will motivate the reader to share life's recipes for spiritual health.

❀ *By being encouraged to induce productive changes in society.* Each woman is unique in age, size, shape, color, and talents. Each

brings her special flavor to the world in her service to God and others. *Sweet Truths* will help each reader to recognize her own potential.

How is the book different from others in its category?
Truths from God's Word are served up in a simple, enjoyable format, handmade by Judi and me, sisters who have experienced these "sweet truths" since childhood. I can imagine the reader's snuggling in front of a cozy fireplace sipping hot cocoa and smiling as she relates to our stories and illustrations and acknowledges the biblical realities.

What scripture best sums up the theme of the book?
James 4:14: "For what is your life? It is even a vapor that appears for a little time and then vanishes away." Chocolate doesn't last long very long in our home. Neither does our pilgrimage on this planet. So we must appreciate life, enjoy it, and share it with others!

What did you learn from studying and researching this topic?

I enjoyed this study as I prepared the same topic for ladies' days. I have learned that, just as Jesus used ordinary comparisons in His daily teaching, we can gain much from relating things that women have in common—a love for chocolate—to many spiritual lessons for daily living!

How do you feel about *Sweet Truths*?

Being a chocolate lover from way back, it was fun to write about the small pleasures found in one of my favorite treats. Women will find it effortless to relate to these comparisons, just as I do. I enjoyed taking the attributes of chocolate and showing through scripture how we can handle the joys and challenges of the Christian life. We covered the bitter and the sweet!

How will the reader benefit from *Sweet Truths*?

❋ Its short chapters will grab attention and enable today's busy women to digest a spiritual nugget that is pleasing and nourishing—and manageable!

❋ Its lesson topics are simple and will have general appeal to a wide audience.

❋ Its various subjects assure that each reader will find comparisons that will hit home. Hopefully, she will gain insight into better handling and acceptance of life's trials.

How is the book different from other books in its category?
It is fun! Jesus said in John 10:10: "I came that you might have life, and have it more abundantly." Jesus wanted us to enjoy the life He gave us. If we live for Him in an enjoyable way, then we truly can experience an abundant life. What's more fun than chocolate?

What scripture best sums up the theme of the book?
Romans 12:2: "Be transformed by the renewing of your mind." When we study principles of God's Word, we train our minds to be more Christ-like. Each chapter holds scripture that will help us transform our lives in a positive way for Christ.

Transforming the Bitter

SWEET TRUTHS

1 Peter 3:3–4

"Do not let your adornment be merely outward— arranging the hair, wearing gold, or putting on fine apparel—rather let it be the hidden person of the heart, with the incorruptible beauty of a gentle and quiet spirit, which is very precious in the sight of God."

Ephesians 4:29

"Let no corrupt word proceed out of your mouth, but what is good for necessary edification, that it may impart grace to the hearers."

Proverbs 31:10, 26

"Who can find a virtuous wife? For her worth is far above rubies . . . She opens her mouth with wisdom, and on her tongue is the law of kindness."

13

Like chocolate, a sweet life requires transformation.

What's Inside?

1. God wants us to transform spiritually.

2. The transformation process may be long, messy, and uncomfortable.

3. People react differently to trials. Some end up bitter. Some end up better.

4. Only through the unique sweetness found in Christ can we help others. (Sometimes we help by refusing to help!)

Law of Kindness

Like chocolate, life requires a transformation process to become sweet. Peter tells us to have a meek and gentle spirit (1 Peter 3:3–4). Proverbs 31:26 urges us to have the law of kindness on our tongues. Sometimes it is hard to be sweet, isn't it? Of course!

❃ When somebody jumps ahead of you in line at the grocery store.

❃ When someone says something uncomplimentary about your child.

❄ When you are at a yard sale and somebody grabs an item you saw first.

❄ When someone starts an untrue rumor about you.

Do these situations call for revenge? No, we are Christians. And when we made the decision to follow Him, we were transformed—we became Christlike.

Paul directs us, "And do not be conformed to this world, but be transformed by the renewing of your mind" (Romans 12:2).

Becoming Sweet

Becoming sweet may be a long and messy transformation process for some new Christians. What a wonderful coincidence—our tasty chocolate bar also experienced a similar metamorphosis! Chocolate in its raw form does not taste anything like the final product. The seeds from a cacao tree are bitter and astringent with a slightly nutty and floral overtone, in texture somewhat like unripe beans. The pulp that surrounds each seed has the flavor of a Sweet Tart. But yuk! Spit out the seeds. Bringing out the wonderful flavor we identify as "Ah, it's chocolate!" is a complex process. The Encarta Online dictionary explains it like this:

Chocolate causes certain endocrine glands to secrete hormones that affect your feelings and behavior by making you happy. Therefore, it counteracts depression, in turn reducing the stress of depression. Your stress-free life helps you maintain a youthful disposition, both physically and mentally. So eat lots of chocolate!

—Elaine Sherman

> Chocolate manufacturers begin with cacao seeds. They are warmed and allowed to ferment in a pulpy state for three to nine days. The seeds dry and turn brown. Enzymes within the pulp are activated to release substances that will later produce the special flavor. The

beans are dried, cleaned, and roasted to bring out that characteristic chocolate flavor. Then they are put into a crushing machine that shells and grinds them into chocolate. During this process, the fat melts and produces a liquid called chocolate liquor. This liquid may be used to make chocolate candy or it may be filtered (removing the fat), cooled, and ground to produce cocoa powder.

> All of the evil that people have thrust upon chocolate is really more deserved by milk chocolate, which is essentially contaminated. The closer you get to a pure chocolate liquor (the chocolate essence ground from roasted cacao beans) the purer it is, the more satisfying it is, the safer it is, and the healthier it is.
>
> —Arnold Ismach, "The Darker Side of Chocolate"

What a long, complex, and messy process to produce this delicious product!

Sometimes we, too, have to go through heated, uncomfortable trials in order to become sweet and lovable. Teddy Copeland's *Playing the Hand You Are Dealt* describes women who have gone through tough times: widowhood, loss of a child, and terminal illness of a loved one. These women confronted difficulties head on and overcame them.

In chapter 13 Teddy relates the event of a woman who dealt with her son's incarceration for illegal alcohol and drug activities. Here is her transformation:

"At first," Darrollene continues, "I thought I could've accepted Ryan's death easier than all this. But now I am so thankful that God gave him another chance. I see now that God knew what was best. All of us are much more spiritual now. I can say from the bottom of my heart that I would do it all again for God to get the glory for the changes I have seen in my family" (Teddy Copeland, *Playing the Hand You Are Dealt*, Lambert Book House, Inc., 1997, page 92).

Our challenge is to accept our sufferings with the attitude of "Why not me?" rather than "Why me?" The Christian woman knows that,

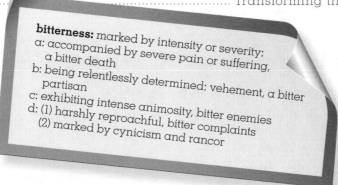

bitterness: marked by intensity or severity:
a: accompanied by severe pain or suffering, a bitter death
b: being relentlessly determined: vehement, a bitter partisan
c: exhibiting intense animosity, bitter enemies
d: (1) harshly reproachful, bitter complaints (2) marked by cynicism and rancor

like chocolate, she can become sweet in the process of being crushed. That is the goal—be sweet, not bitter. James 1:2–5 tells us to count it all joy when trials come to us because they help us to develop patience and Christian maturity. J. B. Phillips translates the text like this:

> When all kinds of trials and temptations crowd into your lives, my [sisters], don't resent them as intruders, but welcome them as friends! Realize that they come to test your faith and to produce in you the quality of endurance. But let the process go on until that endurance is fully developed, and you will find you have become [women] of mature character with the right sort of independence. And if, in the process, any of you does not know how to meet any particular problem, [she] has only to ask God—who gives generously . . . without making [her] feel foolish or guilty—and [she] may be quite sure that the necessary wisdom will be given [her].

Why is it so difficult for us to welcome trials as friends, not intruders? What is our help if we do not know how to meet a problem?

_____

_____

_____

Name one of the strongest, most godly people you know. How did a specific trial influence that person's spirituality?

_____

_____

_____

Carrot, Egg, or Coffee Bean?

Life was not treating Jennifer very well—at least, that's what she thought—so she dressed Sara, jumped into the car, and drove across town to visit the best counselor she knew.

"Mother," she began, after quietly entering the living room she knew so well, "Rob's having to spend a lot more time at the office with his new promotion, Sara's cutting teeth, and my house looks like a train wreck, to say nothing of my hair and nails. When I solve one problem, two more jump into my life. I'm frustrated!"

"Oh, dear," Mother said sympathetically. "Let's go into the kitchen."

Jennifer followed her mother into another very familiar room of her "old" house and dropped into a dining chair, Sara in her lap. Without saying a word, Mother filled three pots with water and set them on burners. The flames leaped under them.

Jennifer watched in silence.

Mother took an egg and a carrot from the refrigerator and dropped them into separate pots. Then she scooped a bit of coffee from a canister and dumped it into the last pot.

Mother pulled out a chair and sat down at the table. They sat in silence. Even Sara was quiet.

The water in all three pots came to a boil. After a few minutes Mother rose from the table, fished the carrot out and into a bowl, broke and peeled the egg, and ladled a bit of coffee into a cup. Then she moved the carrot, egg, and coffee to the table.

"Tell me, Jennifer, what do you see?"

"A carrot, an egg, and coffee," she replied.

"Test the carrot," Mother said.

Jennifer touched it with a fork and lifted it to her mouth. "The hard carrot is now soft," she replied.

"Now test the 'liquid' egg."

Jennifer stuck her fork into it, dug out a bit of yellow, and put it into her mouth. "It's hard-boiled—no longer liquid."

"Now try the coffee."

Jennifer picked up the cup, savored the aroma, and touched her lips to the liquid. "It's rich and delicious," she said. "So what are you telling me, Mother?"

Mother explained, "Each of these objects faced the same adversity—boiling water—but each reacted differently. The carrot was hard and unrelenting, but the boiling water broke down those hard fibers and made the carrot soft.

I don't understand why so many "so called" chocolate lovers complain about the calories in chocolate, when all true chocoholics know that it is a vegetable. It comes from the cocoa bean and beans are veggies. 'Nuff said.

"The eggs were liquid. That thin, fragile shell was their total protection. But after sitting through the boiling water, the insides hardened.

"The situation of the coffee is different. The boiling water seemed strong and independent, but guess what. When it attacked the coffee, the coffee fought back and changed the composition of the water."

Jennifer dropped her head. "I've got it, Mother. Adversity affects people differently—according to the strength of their character."

"So what is your present 'character' status, Jennifer? Is it as strong as it was when you stood strongly for right during your high school years?"

"Mother, it seems I've slipped a bit, but give me a couple of days with my God and His Word and the answer will be yes—even stronger!"

The problem: How to get two pounds of chocolate home from the store in a hot car.

The solution: Eat it in the parking lot.

Which am I? Am I the carrot that seems strong but, with pain and adversity, do I wilt and become soft and lose my strength? Am I the egg that starts with a malleable heart, but changes with the heat? Did I once have a fluid spirit but, after a death, a breakup, or a financial hardship, does my shell now look the same, but on the inside am I bitter and tough with a stiff spirit and a hardened heart?

Or am I the coffee that actually changes the water? Do I interact with the circumstances that bring pain and force them to release their fragrance and flavors?

When the hours are the darkest and trials reach their apex, do you rise to another level? When things are at their worst, if you find strength to change the situation for the better, then you are like the coffee. How do you handle adversity? Are you a carrot, an egg, or a coffee bean?

Everyone has problems: sickness; grief over the loss of a loved one; financial issues; emotional issues of anger, anxiety, or addiction—we could go on and on. Everyone has problems! In fact, some people who seem happiest have more problems than even their friends can imagine. But with God's help, use their problems to transform their lives.

Judi's Sweets

All three of our children were born with physical disabilities. Have they plucked bitterness from life's tree as a result? Read on and see for yourself.

Firstborn son Phil and lastborn daughter Micah have epidermylosis bullosa, a fancy name for a blistering skin disorder. The hereditary birth condition instigates production of only two layers of skin instead of three. Hands and feet blister when exposed to common activities. One or two trips across the monkey bars or one day of sports training may produce blisters that cover the hands and feet. No, not the normal blisters you might get from a new pair of shoes, but quarter-sized sores pushing toes apart.

We have often watched Phil and Micah hobble. They wanted stylish shoes, but their wishes could not always be met. Happily, they could participate in some sports, especially as they got older and learned to maneuver around their challenges.

Garrett, our middle child, has Tourette's syndrome. The condition seems invisible now, since he has outgrown many of the symptoms. But when he was in the fourth and fifth grades, it was a major issue. He would twitch and jerk and make unintelligible noises. Life was rough for him at school, at church, and in general.

I am happy to say that the kids did not let their problems control them. Phil could not excel in sports, but he had no problem sitting still and letting his mind work. He developed a tremendous musical talent.

Sweet Truths

Garrett learned to laugh through the teasing about his twitches and noises and developed a sensitivity that propelled him into social work. Also, the obsessive compulsive disorder that is often associated with Tourette's syndrome helped him in perfecting his basketball and drumming skills.

Because of her challenges in growing up, Micah learned to listen and empathize with others. She was affectionately known by close friends as the "psychologist of Dixon basement" while in college. Later, her compassion and caring attitude led her into a career in a pediatric office.

Through trials, all three of my children became better instead of bitter.

The following responses to trials are found in 1 Corinthians 4:12–13: we labor; we bless; we endure; we entreat. What are the trials? How are these responses both positive and Christlike?

_____

_____

_____

_____

_____

_____

In Ephesians 4:31, bitterness is listed with a host of other sins. Considering the definition given earlier and the sins listed with bitterness, what sinful actions can come out of bitterness?

_____

_____

_____

Exodus 1:14 says that the Egyptians made the lives of the Israelites bitter with hard bondage. How can the actions of other people cause bitterness in us?

_____

_____

How do you respond to trials? Do you look for the good in every situation or do you see only the negative? How can we, with a negative attitude, bring others to Christ? Are they really attracted to Christianity when we send out this message: "Come worship with us. We're a bunch of miserable folks and you can be too! We will help you grow to become like us!" No! Negativity repels; it does not attract.

Someone once said, "You catch more flies with honey than with vinegar." A sweet attitude reflects Christ in our lives. He did not die that we might have a poor, wretched, miserable life. He came that we might have life and "have it more abundantly" (John 10:10). He came

to bring us joy. "Rejoice in the Lord always. Again I will say, rejoice!" (Philippians 4:4).

Read Philippians 4 and note resources that helped Paul to be positive in his poor circumstances, even while he was in a Roman prison.

_____

_____

_____

_____

List two challenges you have faced in the past. Consider your responses. Did you become bitter or better as a result of those experiences?

_____

_____

_____

_____

_____

_____

When we talk with someone who is going through difficult times, we must let our Christian sweetness show. It may be tempting to say, "My aunt died of that" or "You think you've got it bad. When my sister's husband left, she had to . . . " Such calloused emotions turn people off.

> A gentle answer turns away wrath, but a harsh word stirs up anger.
>
> —Proverbs 15:1 NASB

If we want to reach others with the gospel, we must season our words, make them appetizing—like delicious chocolate. Can you imagine that before the 1880s chocolate bars were hard, brittle, and difficult to swallow? Then Rudolphe Lindt of Bern, Switzerland, created a recipe that attracted many to this sweet treat. He added cocoa butter during the manufacturing process. His goal was to make the candy smoother and glossier. But there was a serendipitous result. Cocoa butter melts at human body temperature, 97 degrees Fahrenheit, and therefore, that gentle adjustment made chocolate better—more palatable and more popular. It melts in your mouth!

In the same manner, our words must be softened so they will melt in the hearts of our listeners.

> Let no corrupt word proceed out of your mouth, but what is good for necessary edification, that it may impart grace to the hearers (Ephesians 4:29).

Lost and hurting people need positive words. Like chocolate, they need a little sweetness. We can best serve others only when we have been transformed into the gentle, sweet likeness of Christ.

What are some practical ways we can "be transformed" as we are instructed in Romans 12:2? (Keep in mind that transformation requires a "renewing of the mind.")

_____

_____

_____

_____

In Exodus 15:22–25 the Israelites, three days into the wilderness of Shur, became very thirsty. They were elated to find water—until they tasted it. It was bitter. Moses asked the Lord what to do. The Lord showed him a tree and told him to cast it into the water. Upon doing so, the water became sweet. Explain how applying God's instructions instead of insisting on applying our own solutions can transform bitterness into sweetness.

_____

_____

_____

_____

_____

STIRRING SWEETNESS

1. Reflect on the lives of two godly women who have come through trials and been transformed into sweetness. How was their Christian influence enhanced? How did their experiences impact you? Write them a note of appreciation.

2. Determine to view your own trials in a different light. List some challenges you have experienced, and analyze your response to them in view of the scriptures we have examined this week.

WRAPPING IDEAS

Recipe Book. Bring your favorite chocolate recipe to your ladies' class and appoint a volunteer to put them into book form. Make sure everyone gets a copy. Then make extras to give to visitors, friends, newcomers in the community, and brides-to-be.

Dunca's Divine Divinity Candy

1 cup sugar

3 T corn syrup

⅓ cup water

1 egg white, beaten stiff

⅓ t vanilla

Bring sugar, syrup, and water to soft ball stage, about 230 degrees. Continue cooking, but meanwhile begin to beat egg whites. Stop cooking the candy mixture at hard ball stage, about 255 degrees. Pour mixture slowly with constant beating over egg whites. Beat until it takes shape (a dull gloss appearance). Add vanilla. Using 2 spoons, drop on waxed paper to form triangular-shaped candy.

Mama's Old Fashioned Fudge

¾ cup cocoa
3 cups sugar
1 cup milk
Pinch of salt

Cook these in iron skillet over med-high heat until soft ball forms when dropped in cold water. Remove from heat and add:

½ stick butter
½ bag mini-marshmallows
½ cup nuts
1 t vanilla

Stir quickly and pour into buttered dish. Cut and serve.

Mama's Old Fashioned Fudge (Revised)

Mom used to make this in an iron skillet. She used a cup of milk and put the butter in last. Using that much liquid took about 20 minutes to cook. This is an updated version with ⅓ cup milk. (You get to eat it sooner!)

½ stick of margarine
1 cup sugar
⅓ cup cocoa
⅓ cup milk
½ cup peanut butter
1 t vanilla
Nuts (optional) I use crunchy peanut butter so it has nuts already!

Mix together all except the peanut butter and vanilla. Bring to a boil over med-high heat and cook for 8 minutes or until soft ball forms in cold glass of water. Remove from heat and add peanut butter and vanilla. Stir quickly and pour onto a buttered dinner plate. Let cool and cut into squares. Enjoy!

Eating the Whole Thing

(It's tempting to take it all in at once!)

SWEET TRUTHS

James 4:14 KJV	"For what is your life? It is even a vapour, that appeareth for a little time, and then vanisheth away."
Psalm 46:10	"Be still, and know that I am God."
Jeremiah 29:11–13 ESV	"For I know the plans I have for you, declares the Lord, plans for welfare and not for evil, to give you a future and a hope. Then you will call upon me and come and pray to me, and I will hear you. You will seek me and find me, when you seek me with all your heart."

CENTER

Just like a box of chocolates, it is tempting to take on too much of life at once—even when it's full of good things!

What's  Inside?

1. Hurrying through life causes us to miss life's present joys.

2. Why should we slow down?

3. Observing the main thing—seek first His kingdom—eliminates trivialities.

4. Choosing God's way is best.

Savor the Flavor

Have you ever wanted to eat a whole box of chocolates at one sitting? Of course! It is very tempting, isn't it? Yes, but it robs you of some of the joys of chocolate. You barely enjoy the taste of one before you bite into the next.

Life is like that, too. With so much to do, we sometimes hurry in the present to attempt to get into the future. But somehow we never make it. The future is elusive; the present is always with us.

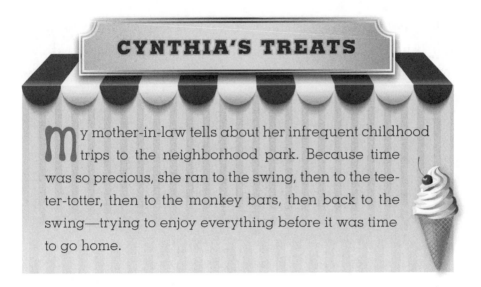

CYNTHIA'S TREATS

my mother-in-law tells about her infrequent childhood trips to the neighborhood park. Because time was so precious, she ran to the swing, then to the tee-ter-totter, then to the monkey bars, then back to the swing—trying to enjoy everything before it was time to go home.

Do you ever find yourself hurrying to get to work, to get your kids to school, to run errands on your lunch break, to pick up the kids, to get them to a ballgame or music practice, to get yourself to a class or a meeting, or to hurry home and prepare dinner? (On that last one, do you just take a short cut through the drive-through?). If you are like us, you sometimes feel as if you are on a high-speed treadmill, screaming, "Please, somebody! Stop this thing for a moment and let me rest!"

Be Still!

It is not always easy to focus on the concept, "For what is your life? It is even a vapour, that appeareth for a little time, and then vanisheth away" (James 4:14 KJV). But the Lord directs us in Psalm 46:10, "Be still, and know that I am God."

An older woman in the Guys' first ministry in Yucaipa, California, lived a powerful example of relishing the present. Sister Counts had what she called "slow me down, Lord" days. Although she was busy—gardening, canning, teaching Bible classes, and serving as an elder's

wife—she occasionally abandoned her time-saving devices to spend time with the Lord. She would hand wash and towel dry her dishes and leisurely hang her clothes on the line. Do you ever need a "slow me down, Lord" day?

Even Jesus took time to get away from it all on a mountain, in a desert, and, yes, even in a garden—the Garden of Gethsemane. What prompted Him to seek solitude?

Matthew 14:10–13 _____

Matthew 14:23 _____

Luke 5:15–16 _____

Eat, Drink, Lie Down to Rest

What might happen to your body if you hurriedly gulped down a whole box of chocolates? You would get sick. Right? Living always in a hurry can have the same effect.

Medical experts advise us not to keep going when our bodies say stop! Those who push themselves beyond their normal limits are prone to illness. They are *stressed;* they truly feel like *desserts* spelled backward!

Our sister Donna loved to go, go, go. When she and her army-sergeant husband lived in Stuttgart, Germany, Donna filled her time designing and making ball gowns for the fancy military dinners. She sometimes stayed up all night to finish sewing on sequins. We lost our sister to leukemia in 1992. This is not to say that her late hours caused her death, but that intense pace could not have helped her healing.

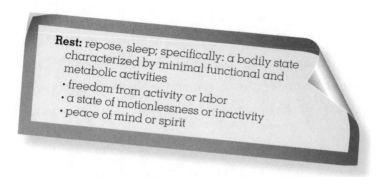

Rest: repose, sleep; specifically: a bodily state characterized by minimal functional and metabolic activities
• freedom from activity or labor
• a state of motionlessness or inactivity
• peace of mind or spirit

God put body clocks inside us to tell us when to stop and rest. We must listen.

Consider Elijah's experience after Mt. Carmel (1 Kings 19:1–8). He had bravely stood up for God, calling down fire from heaven. The people believed and shouted, "The Lord, He is God!" (1 Kings 18:39). But when Queen Jezebel became enraged over the loss of her prophets, she threatened to kill him. He ran. He went a day's journey into the wilderness and lay under a broom tree, praying that he might die.

I could give up chocolate but I'm not a quitter.

"It is enough!" he said, "Now, Lord, take my life, for I am no better than my fathers!" (1 Kings 19:4). He was exhausted and depressed. God then gave the perfect prescription for burn-out. An angel of the Lord told him, "Arise and eat." Elijah obeyed. And then he lay down to rest.

The angel returned, touched him, and said, "Arise and eat, because the journey is too great for you." He again arose and ate and drank. Then he went in the strength of that food for forty days and nights as far as Horeb, the mountain of God.

We hurry through life. We overdo. Then "the journey is too great" for us (1 Kings 19:7). We desperately need to slow down and balance our activities.

When we open that wonderful box of chocolates, it is better to eat one or two pieces and savor the flavor slowly. (Chocoholics are allowed three or four!) And, of course, remember to eat the best piece first, so you can truly enjoy its sweetness before your appetite is dulled!

Consider your personal schedule. Too full? What are some changes you can make to slow down?

_____

_____

What Is His Plan?

We have more peace when we follow Jesus' example of seeking solitude. Sadly, we plan our lives with too many things on our "to do" list. Judi has heard her preacher husband, Stan, repeat, "Learn to say no even to some good things so you can say yes to better things."

Today's culture bombards us to be super-women and super-moms. And we can do it all! Our problem is that there is so much we *can* be involved in that we sometimes forget what we *should* be involved in.

Do we ever stop to think about God's plan for us? If so, why do we often seem to squeeze Him out by trying to take everything in all at once? Then we decide that if we have some time left over, we will give that to God.

What's the best chocolate? The one we are eating!

34

"For I know the plans that I have for you," declares the Lord, "plans for welfare and not for calamity to give you a future and a hope" (Jeremiah 29:11 NASB).

You might say, "Well, you don't live in *my* world. I'm too busy. I don't have enough time." Be honest. How often do you say, "I'm too busy"? Sometimes we are busy, but if we are too busy to do the Lord's work, then we are too busy—period!

What Bible character said he would call for spiritual help in a "more convenient season"? (Acts 24). Discuss his situation and compare to present-day lack of prioritizing.

_____

_____

_____

_____

_____

_____

Perhaps we need to learn to use in a better way the time the Lord has given us. At the office we feel obligated to spend our time doing the work the boss has assigned. We are "on the boss's clock."

So consider this: God has put us in charge of some things here on earth. We are on His clock. We must not cheat Him. We must not come in late or check out early.

What Is My Plan?

Our biggest problem in arranging time to do God's work may be that we fail to consider His work when we make our schedules. Then later, in emergency fashion, we try to crowd it in. It doesn't fit. We have forced God's work to take a back seat to the mundane.

Try an experiment using the following materials:

1. Glass jar

2. Large marbles

3. BBs

4. Sand

5. Water

6. Tennis ball

Take a glass container, like a fishbowl or a wide-mouth quart jar. Fill it half full of sand. Then fill the remainder half full of BBs. Fill to the top with large marbles. Pour in water to settle the ingredients. The tennis ball? There's no room for it. It will have to sit on top, outside the jar.

Stress wouldn't be so difficult if it came chocolate covered.

Retry the experiment using the same materials in the same quantities. Just be sure to put the tennis ball in first. Then add the large marbles. Add the BBs. Add the sand. Now pour in the water. Got it! It all fits because all the crevices are filled.

Consider this in light of our spiritual priorities. We must put that most important item on our "to do" list first and make sure it takes priority. Then the less important items will fit nicely around it.

We must plan to serve God. We must give His work first place in our schedules and then work everything else around it! Plan to be present when the church meets. Plan to get involved in the works the elders have set forth in the congregation. Plan to spend time in personal study and prayer. Then everything else will work around God's schedule.

> Seek those things which are above, where Christ is, sitting at the right hand of God. Set your mind on things above, not on things on the earth (Colossians 3:1–2).

What is the common phrase in 1 Chronicles 22:19 and 2 Chronicles 11:16? How does this phrase apply to you today?

_____

_____

We must get our priorities right. Reaching for a box of chocolates every time we get hungry will not satisfy our dietary needs. Even worse, the temporary satisfaction we experience will be detrimental to our health. Jesus' words are the bread and living water for which we hunger and thirst (John 6; 7:37–38).

> A chocolate in the mouth is worth two on the plate.

If we fill up on junk, we will not have an appetite for the good stuff. In true likeness, if we fill our schedules with our own plans, why would we long for God's plans?

How many hours do I have every day? List one action that will help me guarantee that I incorporate Bible study and at least one act of kindness into every day.

_____

_____

Guidance, Satisfaction, and Strength

If we want to learn God's plan for us and enjoy a long, full life, we must remember to slow down, be still, and know that He is.

> The Lord will guide you continually, and satisfy your soul in drought, and strengthen your bones; you shall be like a watered garden, and like a spring of water, whose waters do not fail (Isaiah 58:11).

STIRRING SWEETNESS

1. Consider biblical examples of people who took on too many duties. (Moses' judging the people, Exodus 18:13–27; Martha distracted with much serving, Luke 10:40). Did they solve their time problems? If so, how?

2. What will make it easier to say no to too many activities?

WRAPPING IDEAS

Group project: Have a chocolate pajama party! Everyone must wear something brown or white to symbolize brown or white chocolate. Bring a one-dollar gift that is brown or white. Bring a chocolate snack. Play your favorite games to exchange the one-dollar gifts so that everyone has someone else's gift. Enjoy your snacks, and take time to discuss how each person's Christian life is like a box of chocolates.

Nanny Redden's Mounds Cake

1 Devil's food cake mix (no pudding in mix)

Filling:

1 cup sugar

1 cup milk

1 stick margarine

30 large marshmallows

1 T vanilla

1 14 oz pkg coconut

Icing:

1 stick margarine

3 T cocoa

½ cup milk

1 lb powdered sugar

1 cup chopped nuts

1 T vanilla

Bake cake according to directions on box in 2 round cake pans (8 or 9 in). Turn out and cool. Slice each layer crosswise into 2 layers, making 4 in all.

Make filling:

Boil sugar, milk, and margarine 10 minutes or until syrupy. Turn off burner and stir in marshmallows until dissolved. Add vanilla and coconut. Put this mixture between layers of cake.

Make Icing:

Mix margarine, cocoa, and milk in saucepan and boil for 3 minutes. Remove from heat and add powdered sugar. Mix well. Add nuts and vanilla. Beat until smooth. Spread on top and sides of cake working from the bottom up so you won't tear up the layers.

Virginia's Chocolate Cobbler

1½ sticks margarine

2½ cups sugar (divided)

7 T cocoa (divided)

1 t vanilla

2½ cups milk (divided)

¾ cup water

1½ cups self-rising flour

Melt margarine in 9 x 13 oven dish. Combine 1 cup sugar, 1½ cups flour, 3 T cocoa, 1 t vanilla and 1 cup milk. Pour this mixture over butter. DO NOT STIR after you pour it on! Mix together 1½ cups sugar, 4 T cocoa. Sprinkle over mixture. DO NOT STIR!

Heat 1½ cups milk and ¾ cup water.

Pour over entire mixture trying to wet it all. DO NOT STIR!

Bake at 350 for 30 minutes.

It might look like it is not done, but it is. Let it set about 15 minutes. It will form a cake in the middle with pudding around and under it!

DELICIOUS!

This recipe came from Judi's sweet mother-in-law, Virginia Dean Masonia. A favorite at potlucks!

Sharing the Sweetness

SWEET TRUTHS

1 Corinthians 15:58

"Therefore, my beloved brethren, be steadfast, immovable, always abounding in the work of the Lord, knowing that your labor is not in vain in the Lord."

• •

Philippians 2:4

"Let each of you look out not only for his own interests, but also for the interests of others."

• •

Ephesians 2:28 NASB

. . . He must labor, performing with his own hands what is good, so that he will have something to share with one who has need.

CENTER

True Christianity involves sharing our lives with those around us.

What's Inside?

1. Sharing with others may take us out of our comfort zones.

2. We have many opportunities to share our lives in service.

3. We must listen to others and consider their needs.

4. We are to be doing Christ's work until He returns.

Someone once said, "Sorrow can be borne alone; but joy must be shared." Mark Twain put it this way: "To get the full value of joy, you must have someone to divide it with." Sharing our chocolates brings joy to others and to us. If we receive a box of chocolates and do not share, we are missing a blessing! Likewise, sharing our lives brings joys to others; it also brings joy to us!

> Giving chocolate to others is an intimate form of communication, a sharing of deep, dark secrets.
>
> —Milton Zelman, publisher of "Chocolate News"

CYNTHIA'S TREATS

On Sundays, my husband, Steven, enjoys circulating around in the auditorium, talking to members and visitors before and after worship and Bible class. Although I am not as much a people person as he, I follow his lead and mingle. A part of me sometimes wants to arrive just in time for worship to begin and quietly sit in the pew as many others do. But that is not what Jesus would do. He would consider all the lonely people there: widows, single moms, and grieving, depressed, and hurting people.

Don't we all need the smiles and cheerful hellos that can be shared, even if they put us out of our comfort zones? If we stay in our own little world—pew—and never become involved with others, we become lonely and selfish. As with chocolate, a Christlike life is made for sharing.

Being part of a congregation offers many opportunities to reach out. There are always people who need meals: the sick, the shut-ins, and those coming home from the hospital. Matthew 25 informs us that when we take food, we will hear Jesus say, "I was hungry and you fed me." However, many women turn down requests to take food to the hurting and needy. Have you ever offered excuses such as "I don't have time" or "I don't know that person"?

The following poem has been circulated through church bulletins for years. We do not know who wrote it, but we found Gus Nichols' name with it in one bulletin. The poem represents one who learned the blessings of sharing her life with others through food service:

What nerve! What gall!
For Mrs. Whatsit to call!
I don't even know the one who died,
And the family at church, I never spied!
Now I wouldn't mind to open a can,
If it were someone I know like Ann or Dan.
Why I've got washin' and ironin' to do,
Shoppin' and bakin' and cleanin' too.
Ask someone else to do that chore,
I've got all I can do and more.

These words ring clear in my ears,
And cut at my heart like a pair of shears.
You see—last week my loved one died,
And I needed a friend by my side.
Mrs. Whatsit was the first to drop by,
With words of comfort and an apple pie.
Others came in a steady flow.
People from church whom I didn't even know.
They came with food and a sympathetic smile.
Some took time to talk awhile.

I've asked God to forgive me for my lack of love,
And pray for His blessings from above.
For never again will it be a bother
To take a dish in the name of my Father.

If a Christian's life is worth anything, she must share it. The Bible says so: "Be steadfast, immovable, always *abounding* [emphasis ours] in the work of the Lord" (1 Corinthians 15:58). How can we share? We do it the same way Christ did it while He was here. After all, we are His body and we are to continue His work. Let's look at His example:

1. He spent time teaching the lost.

2. He spent time comforting.

3. He spent time encouraging.

4. He spent time with children.

> There's nothing better than a good friend, except a good friend with chocolate.
> —Linda Grayson,
> *"The Pickwick Papers"*

5. He spent time strengthening the faith of believers.

6. He spent time setting an example.

Look at all the things women can do in the church, things Jesus needs us to do until He returns.

One of the big jobs we can fill is to teach children's Bible classes. We may never know the impact we have on a child's future.

Judi's Sweets

Of all the Bible students I have taught, my favorites are fifth-graders. They are at a pivotal point in life. The world throws so much at them: school, sports, fitting in, fashion, materialism, peer pressure. They are discovering who they are and who they want to be. Fifth grade is an ideal time to ground them in Bible basics that will serve as the foundation of their faith. They are usually quick to grasp the plan of salvation.

Are you a teacher? If so, you are probably familiar with the adage: *The teacher learns the most.* That is true because good teachers are ever-learning pupils! What a great way to share your Christian life. If you don't feel you can teach, contact the education director and apply to be a co-teacher. Then while you help children learn, you can learn from a master teacher.

The classroom is not the only place to teach. Wives teach and convert husbands. Parents teach children. Christians teach friends and co-workers. Neighbors teach neighbors. Comment underneath each of the following references regarding teaching the lost effectively:

Even if some do not obey the word, they, without a word, may be won by the conduct of their wives (1 Peter 3:1).

_____

_____

Go therefore and make disciples of all the nations, baptizing them in the name of the Father and of the Son and of the Holy Spirit, teaching them to observe all things that I have commanded you (Matthew 28:19–20).

_____

_____

> Which of these three, do you think, proved to be a neighbor to the man who fell among the robbers?" He said, "The one who showed him mercy." And Jesus said to him, "You go, and do likewise" (Luke 10:36–37 ESV).

_____

_____

Let's not forget our elderly. Sometimes we get caught up in our own little world and assume that someone else is taking care of the older members. Philippians 2:4 says, "Let each of you look out not only for his own interests, but also for the interests of others." Have you ever considered that many elderly people have lost the love of their lives? If your husband is still living, can you imagine life without him? When you go out with your friends, do you think about the older brothers and sisters who have lost close friends?

When you are driving to a restaurant, does it ever cross your mind that many in our older generation no longer have driving privileges? Make an effort to share time with them.

> All I really need is love, but a little chocolate now and then doesn't hurt!
>
> —Lucy Van Pelt
> (in *Peanuts*, by
> Charles M. Schulz)

share: to divide and parcel out in shares; apportion
- to participate in, use, enjoy, or experience jointly or in turns
- to relate (a secret or experience, for example) to another or others
- to accord a share in (something) to another or others

47

CYNTHIA'S TREATS

Our ladies' Bible class plans lunch out every Wednesday. Many of the women, especially the elderly, look forward to that event. The men are not left out! The preacher and some of the widowers eat lunch together every Tuesday. The men take turns choosing the restaurant and really enjoy the fellowship.

The Feeble Knees

An elderly gentleman was waiting in a doctor's office for his appointment.

He addressed the nurse: "Miss, it's past time for my appointment, and I must leave here by eleven."

"Dr. Jones is running behind schedule today, Robert. You might need to change your next appointment."

He replied, "Oh, no. I have a standing appointment with my wife. You see, she is in the nursing home and I feed her lunch every day."

"That's kind of you. How is she doing?" the nurse genuinely extended her sympathy.

"Well, she has Alzheimer's and sometimes she doesn't know who I am."

"If she doesn't know you, why is it so important to visit her?"

"Because I still know who she is!"

Perhaps the elderly don't know us, but we know them. Shouldn't we let them know we still recognize them? Most likely, we will all be older one day. Imagine outliving friends and spouse. The days take on sameness unless visitors brighten the door. As Christian sisters, our days are more blessed when we reach out to victims of withering bodies and minds.

"Therefore strengthen the hands which hang down, and the feeble knees" (Hebrews 12:12). Study this passage in context. How does it apply to you?

_____

_____

Think of older folks who may be lonely. Write at least two of their names below. Beside each name, write an action of encouragement. Then do it.

Name _____

Name _____

Bereavement

Another way we can share is by giving encouragement. Just being there for our fellow Christians can make a difference. You may say, "I don't know what to say." Neither did Job's friends. So they sat silently with him for a week (Job 2:13). That was when they were most helpful.

49

What they did say when they opened their mouths should tell us that sometimes it is better to say nothing at all. Just a hug and a smile can encourage.

What can you do when someone loses a loved one?

- ❀ Make a cake.
- ❀ Keep the children.
- ❀ Sit with the sick.
- ❀ Be a face in the crowd at the funeral.
- ❀ Sing at the funeral.
- ❀ Send a card.
- ❀ Make a call.
- ❀ Encourage.

Divorce

Judi's Sweets

One of my good friends called me the day her divorce became final. She said, "I feel like such a failure"—even though she was innocent. What should I say? Should I tell her how much better off she is or what a scoundrel her ex-husband is? No! She is still in love with him; she can't grasp reality on a moment's notice.

I listened as I considered her embarrassment when she appears in public alone, the questions she is asked, and her feelings of being left out of the couples' group at church. Her entire world has turned upside down. I thought, "She needs encouragement."

Have you considered the feelings of one rejected by a spouse? She needs people. Take her to lunch. Plan a shopping trip. (You might finish the day with a chocolate ice cream sundae.) Gather a group of ladies and plan a weekend trip! Good clean fun distracts and encourages a downcast spirit. Remember, Ephesians 4:29 urges us to use the mouth for "edification, that it may impart grace to the hearers." Edification means building up one another. Our friends who have been rejected are broken down and need building up!

Imagine being rejected by your spouse. Describe your feelings. What Bible characters can lend you strength? What scripture will bring you comfort?

_____

_____

Sharing Is Serving

What would you think of a person's sitting in front of you with an open box of chocolates—not sharing? Lonely. And she would be selfish! We must develop a servant attitude. It is not easy to sit with someone at the hospital. It takes time and patience—and sometimes even a strong stomach! You may feel awkward visiting someone who has just lost a loved one. Go anyway! Your presence says a lot. Job's friends helped the most when they sat silently with him (Job 2:13).

Nobody knows the truffles I've seen!

Some acts of service require time and effort. But that's what we are called to do.

Let's listen to one another as a congregation and serve generously. When we serve, we are sharing ourselves—our lives! Christ shared His life, and He asks us to carry on His work until He comes again.

STIRRING SWEETNESS

1. What talents do you possess for sharing Christianity?

2. Discuss some unforgettable acts of service others have done for you.

3. Compare our service to others with Christ's service while on earth.

WRAPPING IDEAS

Cookie Capers. This activity is a hit with teens, but it can be adapted to fit any group. Each person brings a batch of cookies which are divided onto serving plates and covered with plastic wrap. Group members travel to pre-selected homes, put the cookies on the doorstep, ring the doorbell, and run! They leave a note on the cookies: *You have been struck by the Cookie Capers.*

—Youth Group, City, State

Note: Credit for this idea goes to the youth group of Killen Church of Christ, Killen, Alabama.

Handing Down the Recipes

Deuteronomy 6:5–7

"You shall love the Lord your God with all your heart, with all your soul, and with all your strength. And these words which I command you today shall be in your heart. You shall teach them diligently to your children, and shall talk of them when you sit in your house, when you walk by the way, when you lie down, and when you rise up."

Proverbs 4:20–27

"My son, give attention to my words; incline your ear to my sayings. Do not let them depart from your eyes; keep them in the midst of your heart . . . Keep your heart with all diligence, for out of it spring the issues of life. Put away from you a deceitful mouth . . . Let your eyes look straight

53

ahead . . . Ponder the path of your feet, and let all your ways be established. Do not turn to the right or the left; remove your foot from evil."

• •

2 Timothy 1:5

"When I call to remembrance the genuine faith that is in you, which dwelt first in your grandmother Lois and your mother Eunice, and I am persuaded is in you also."

CENTER

God requires us to pass His Word to future generations.

What's Inside?

1. We are responsible for passing God's Word on to others.

2. We must spend time together to pass on values.

3. We need to be careful of worldly influences.

In the Stomach / In the Heart

Do you have a favorite family chocolate recipe? We do and have passed down our mother's fudge recipe so our children can make it in their own kitchens. Today's chocolate companies must also pass on the recipes for their candies or else our grandchildren won't be able to enjoy the delicious chocolate bars we do. Each generation delights in passing on chocolate knowledge so the recipes can remain alive.

> If not for chocolate, there would be no need for control top pantyhose. An entire garment industry would be devastated.

The same is true with spiritual wisdom. We want our children and grandchildren to have a happy, spiritually healthy existence. How can we ensure that?

God presented a recipe through Moses, making it plain that parents must first be examples.

Hear, O Israel: The Lord our God, the Lord is one! You shall love the Lord your God with all your heart, with all your soul, and with all your strength. And these words which I command you today shall be in your heart. You shall teach them diligently to your children, and shall talk of them when you sit in your house, when you walk by the way, when you lie down, and when you rise up (Deuteronomy 6:4–7).

Morning and Night

Parents and grandparents must love God and have a genuine faith in Him before they can pass on a proper respect for God. They must know and obey God's words. Then, according the above recipe, they

are equipped for the discipline of constantly reminding their children of their Creator and Master. When grownups recognize God's power in front of their children, how will it affect those little ones? They will understand that everyone is following the directive of the living God. Children who are taught with this tried and true recipe recognize and respect authority.

CYNTHIA'S TREATS

Steven and I took Deuteronomy 6:4–7 literally. I put the children to bed with Bible stories and he taught them the Bible books and themes in the mornings while blow-drying their hair.

Judi's Sweets

My son Phil says he still remembers that our home-made Bible flash cards had the questions in purple marker on one side and the answers in orange marker on the back. We used those before bedtime each night.

Find an example of handing down truth to children in Joshua 4. Summarize.

_____

_____

_____

How will you begin today to influence the children in your life with the spiritual recipe in Deuteronomy 6?

_____

_____

Doorposts and Gates

The spiritual recipe continues:

> You shall bind them as a sign on your hand, and they shall be as frontlets between your eyes. You shall write them on the doorposts of your house and on your gates (Deuteronomy 6:8–9).

A mother decorated her house with pictures of sailboats, battleships, and other naval vessels. Then she wondered why her boys joined the navy. What pictures and words adorn your home?

When we were young, our mother hung a picture of Jesus in the hall between our bedrooms. Is it a coincidence that both of us married preachers and are now spending our lives in the Lord's ministry?

Surroundings do affect children's thoughts. This explains why teachers spend time making bulletin boards.

Write two ideas for your environment that will influence your children's souls.

_____

_____

Choices for Generations

Did you know that a mother's faith, or lack of it, will affect her descendants for three or four generations? After breaking the tables of stone God made, Moses hewed out two more and returned to the mountain. The Lord passed before him and proclaimed,

> The Lord is longsuffering, and of great mercy, forgiving iniquity and transgression, and by no means clearing the guilty, visiting the iniquity of the fathers upon the children unto the third and fourth generation (Numbers 14:18; Exodus 34:7 KJV).

On the other hand, in 2 Kings 10:30 the Lord explains to Jehu,

> Because thou hast done well in executing that which is right in mine eyes, and hast done unto the house of Ahab according to all that was in mine heart, thy children of the fourth generation shall sit on the throne of Israel. (See also 2 Kings 15:12 KJV.)

Our great-grandfather, Elam "Church" Wilhite, preached the gospel from the "spit and whittle" corner in front of the courthouse in Coopers Chapel, Texas. He and Great-Grandmama Louella influenced their eleven children for Christ. Their youngest is our ninety-six-year-old grandmother Julia, and she still attends worship regularly. Doris, Julia's oldest, is our mother. She has been a great influence in her local congregation for more than forty years.

We are of that fourth generation. Both of us feel a great responsibility to continue that spiritual heritage by raising our children in the Lord. We also spend time teaching our grandchildren. In this way, we will influence our future great-grandchildren.

Influence of Women

Paul's second letter to Timothy presents an excellent example of faith being passed through three generations. Paul wrote to Timothy,

> When I call to remembrance the genuine faith that is in you, which dwelt first in your grandmother Lois and your mother Eunice, and I am persuaded is in you also . . . (2 Timothy 1:5).

You can say this for ready-mixes—the next generation isn't going to have any trouble making pies exactly like mother used to make.

—Earl Wilson

We know a lot about Lois. *How can that be?* you say. *She's mentioned only one time in scripture.* Yes, but have you noticed that Timothy's father was not a Christian? And have you noticed that Lois's daughter Eunice is a Christian and she and Lois are credited for instilling "genuine faith" in Timothy? Have you noticed that Timothy came to be Paul's son in the faith, even though Paul was not his first teacher? The women in Timothy's life showed wisdom in giving him roots and wings in the gospel.

Some women long to be teachers of great crowds while they neglect the obvious—the innocent faces they wash every day. Children are pliable and eager to please. Women with no children often fail to see the potential of their influence—one child who wouldn't have made it without them, now a gospel preacher, a Bible teacher, or an elder's wife.

Tony was one on those children, a child who seemed to have no hope in the Lord. His life was changed because of a neighbor, one woman.

The Joy Bus stopped for the first time at seven-year-old Tony's house. He made the wide stretch up the steps with eagerness because his neighbor Miss Ruth promised him she would be waiting for him as he stepped from the bus. He had lived every day of the past week on that promise. She was waiting for him all right, and Tony was wide-eyed.

But no! The room was strange, and all the children were laughing and talking and having a good time. Miss Betty was there, too, with a quiet smile for Tony. But they were all strangers, except Miss Ruth, who helped Tony to an unfamiliar chair and introduced him to the class. He smiled timidly, gained a little courage, and began to relax a bit.

> Man cannot live on chocolate alone; but woman sure can.

"Class, it's time for the 'Bible Facts' drill," Miss Ruth said, "Who was the first man?" Every hand went up—except Tony's. Miss Ruth asked Melody to answer. "Adam," she said with assurance. Miss Betty gave her a special happy-face sticker.

"Who built the ark?" Miss Ruth asked. All hands went up. Tony squirmed. This time Miss Betty awarded an animal sticker.

Now Miss Ruth turned to him. "Tony, what was the name of the giant David slew?"

"Jesus!" Tony responded with confidence. The class laughed. Tony didn't know the answer. He thought "Jesus" would fit. That was all he knew about the Bible—just "Jesus."

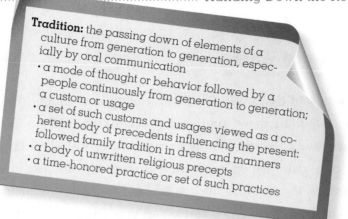

Tradition: the passing down of elements of a culture from generation to generation, especially by oral communication
- a mode of thought or behavior followed by a people continuously from generation to generation; a custom or usage
- a set of such customs and usages viewed as a coherent body of precedents influencing the present: followed family tradition in dress and manners
- a body of unwritten religious precepts
- a time-honored practice or set of such practices

But Tony was blessed far more than he imagined, because Miss Ruth was a wise woman.

Tony was back the next Sunday, and Miss Ruth turned to him to answer the first question.

"Tony, who was the Son of God?"

"Jesus," he replied.

"That is correct, Tony!" Tony beamed and Miss Betty gave him a sticker with a big shiny star.

> Chocolate:
>
> Here today . . .
>
> Gone today!

After a few more questions, Miss Ruth turned again to Tony: "Who was in the temple talking with great teachers when he was only twelve?"

"Jesus," he answered. Another precious sticker!

For several Sundays Tony's "Jesus" answers earned him a string of stickers. And what did Tony think of Miss Ruth's Bible class? No one could keep him away!

Because of one woman, one child received praise and encouragement. Tony soon knew the answers to every question in the Bible drill.

Tony is now a gospel preacher!

Look at your little ones as Lois and Eunice looked at their little Timothy.

Catch Good Values

It is often said that values are more caught than taught. For that to happen, we must spend time with our children and grandchildren. In years gone by, young boys went to the fields with their fathers and the young girls helped mothers with laundry and cleaning. That was just the way of life. Children learned to pattern their lives after their parents. Good morals and values were caught through everyday experiences.

Today, most families are pulled in many directions: Dad working here, Mom working there, and kids attending practices, games, and performances. Stop and consider how much time you actually spend with your family, not just in the same house together, but in interaction, not watching TV together, but talking.

It is sad that so much of what our children "catch" are values coming from the world instead of from godly parents. Here is a bit of information from A. C. Nielsen Company:

The average American watches more than four hours of TV each day. That is 28 hours a week, equivalent to two months of nonstop TV-watching per year! Before retirement at 65, that person will have spent nine years glued to the tube.

Take a look at these alarming TV statistics which influence our children:

* The average child spends 1,680 minutes per week watching television.

* Parents spend only about 3.5 minutes per week in meaningful conversation with their children.

❄ When asked to choose between watching TV and spending time with their fathers, 54 percent of 4- to 6-year-olds preferred television.

❄ The average American youth spends 900 hours per year in school, but watches television 1500 hours a year.

❄ More than 4,000 studies examining TV's effects on children proved that an average child sees over 8,000 murders by the time he finishes elementary school and over 200,000 violent acts by age 18.

CYNTHIA'S TREATS

Two of our sons and their wives chose not to sub-cribe to cable TV. They influenced us to do the same. When you think about it, TV really doesn't offer much worth watching, and it's a distraction from many good things.

How can you help your children to "catch" more spiritual values? List one action you can eliminate and one action you can use to replace it.

_____

_____

Taking Time

Proverbs 4:20–27 reminds us of the children's song, "O Be Careful Little Eyes What You See." It reads,

> My son, give attention to my words; incline your ear to my sayings. Do not let them depart from your sight; keep them in the midst of your heart. For they are life to those who find them and health to all their body. Watch over your heart with all diligence, for from it flow the springs of life. Put away from you a deceitful mouth and put devious speech far from you. Let your eyes look directly ahead and let your gaze be fixed straight in front of you. Watch the path of your feet and all your ways will be established. Do not turn to the right nor to the left; Turn your foot from evil (Proverbs 4:20-27 NASB).

Caution is required in what we hear, what we say, what we do, and where we go.

Parents, before children are old enough to decide for themselves, we have a responsibility to guide their feet, hands, eyes, ears, and mouths. Be careful what you let into your children's world, because they will be influenced by it! And what they learn will be passed on to generations after them. What can be more important?

How are the wise words of Solomon "health to all their body"? (Proverbs 4:22 NASB).

_____

_____

A Parable

An education director, in search of teachers for children, approached some of the more mature members asking them to fill the position. He received a consistent response: "I am enrolled in a class with a wonderful teacher, and the fellowship is superb. I just don't want to leave it." How strange. The drug pusher says, "Not even the threat of jail will keep me from working with your children."

Other adults who were asked to teach said, "I don't have time." But the drug pusher and the porno book dealer said, "We'll stay open from before daylight until the wee hours of the morning—including Sunday!—to win the minds of your kids."

Still other adults said, "I'm unsuited, untrained, and unable to work with children." But the movie producer said, "We will conduct thorough surveys, study passionately, and spend millions of dollars to produce whatever turns your kids on."

This guy found a bottle on the ocean, and he opened it and out popped a genie who gave him three wishes. The guy wished for a million dollars, and poof! There was a million dollars. Then he wished for a convertible, and poof! There was a convertible. And then, he wished he could be irresistible to all women. Poof! He turned into a box of chocolates.

So the adults stayed in their classes where they could enjoy fellowship and increase their Bible knowledge. Not only would they not be tied down on weekends, they also would not be obligated to intensive preparation for a Bible class during the week.

But Sunday came—that first Sunday after the drive to find a teacher. No one was there to teach the children. Everyone assumed that someone would surely fill that position soon. But no one did. The children soon quit coming because they had gone to listen to others who cared about what they did and what went into their minds.

—Selected

What teachings are you passing down to your children?
How are you taking God's instructions seriously, realizing
that your children are young and impressionable only for
a little while?

Did you know that only one in four children brought up in Christian homes remains faithful to the Lord as an adult? How are your habits affecting that statistic? Will the fruits of your labors increase or decrease the "one in four"? Parents, we must pass on God's Word to future generations.

STIRRING SWEETNESS

1. Name some values your parents/grandparents passed down to you.

2. List some character traits you want your children and grandchildren to develop.

3. Discuss creative ways to pass down values and to teach character traits.

4. Monitor your family time for one month and see how much time you are actually spending together.

WRAPPING IDEAS

1. *Activity.* Plan a day to invite the teen girls—or even pre-teen girls—to your house to teach them how to cook homemade fudge or chocolate pie or cake. During their visit, take time to talk about God as well as other truths discussed in this book.

2. *Transform your time.* Turn off the TV for one week. Plan special family activities during TV time. At the end of the week, report on the family atmosphere during TV shutdown.

Kathy's No Crust Fudge Pie

3 eggs

1 cup sugar

¼ cup flour

Pinch of salt

½ cup butter

6 T cocoa

1 t vanilla

½ to 1 cup nuts

Beat eggs until light and fluffy. Mix sugar, flour, and salt and add to eggs. Melt butter and cocoa and add all this to the mixture. Add vanilla and nuts. Grease Pyrex pie pan and pour in mixture. Cook at 350 degrees for 20 minutes—NO LONGER! Serve with whipped cream or ice cream.

Hope's Crowd-Pleaser Chocolate Sheet Cake

2 sticks butter

4 T cocoa

1 cup water

2 cups sugar

2 cups flour, sifted

¼ t salt

½ cup buttermilk

2 eggs, slightly beaten

1 t soda

1 t cinnamon

1 t vanilla

Mix butter, cocoa, and water in a sauce pan and bring to a rapid boil. Combine sifted flour, sugar, and salt in a bowl. Pour butter, cocoa, and water mixture over ingredients in the bowl. Mix well. Add buttermilk, eggs, soda, cinnamon, and vanilla. Mix well. Bake in greased cookie sheet with sides (16 x 11) at 400 degrees for 20 minutes. (Cake may be baked in 9 x 13 cake pan for 40 to 50 minutes.) Spread icing while hot.

Icing

1 stick butter

4 T cocoa

6 T milk

1 lb box powdered sugar

1 t vanilla

pinch of salt

1 cup chopped pecans (optional)

Begin to make 5 minutes before cake is done. Melt margarine and add cocoa and milk. Bring to a boil and remove from heat. Add powdered sugar, vanilla, salt, and nuts. Mix well and spread on hot cake.

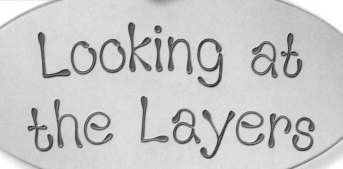

Looking at the Layers

Luke 2:52	"And Jesus increased in wisdom and stature, and in favor with God and men."
Titus 2:3–4	"The older women likewise, that they be reverent in behavior, not slanderers, not given to much wine, teachers of good things—that they admonish the young women to love their husbands, to love their children."
Proverbs 16:31	"The silver-haired head is a crown of glory, if it is found in the way of righteousness."

CENTER

Life offers us different opportunities during each stage.

What's  Inside?

Like a box of chocolates, our lives are divided into layers.

1. Our first twenty years

2. Our second twenty years

3. Our third twenty years

4. At the end, an empty box

Life's Layers

Have you ever received a layered box of chocolates? The most tempting chocolates are packed that way! And it should be no surprise that women's lives are generally made up of three layers.

> **Mature:** having reached full natural growth or development:
> of, relating to, or characteristic of full development, either mental or physical

First Twenty Years

A woman usually spends her first twenty years developing physically, socially, intellectually, and spiritually. Luke 2:52 explains that Jesus did this: "He increased in wisdom [intellectually] and stature [physically] and in favor with God [spiritually] and man [socially]."

CYNTHIA'S TREATS

As a ninth grader, I perceived myself as an ugly duckling, but I found help. Our wise mother bought a subscription to the *Christian Teenager* for Judi, Donna, and me. In one particular article, the author urged each reader to display a photo of herself in her room, put a sticky note on each corner of the photo, and label four areas for personal development: spiritual, physical, social, and intellectual. The author further suggested spending an hour a day: fifteen minutes in prayer and Bible study, fifteen minutes in physical exercise, fifteen minutes studying social graces, and fifteen minutes—or more, as assigned—in school homework. After four years, my ugly-duckling image had disappeared. I graduated high school feeling like a swan.

Judi's Sweets

I still have a poster that Mom made for our teenage girls' class. It features a picture from a magazine of a girl in one corner. The rest of the poster includes cutouts of make-up items. Here is the twist: Mom labeled each product with a spiritual quality:

Lotion bottle: Love—it softens.
Eye shadow: Wisdom—it brightens the eyes.
Shampoo: Study—it cleanses the head.
Perfume: Meekness—it smells sweetly of humility.
Toothpaste & Mouthwash: Kindness—it sweetens the speech.
Blush: Modesty—it gives a great glow.
Lipstick: Encouraging words—they give grace to the hearer.
Foundation: Knowledge—it gives a good base.
Nail Polish: Gentleness—it's great for old or young.

The poster is now yellow and torn, but the words continue to live on, lively and bright in my heart. I treasure these attributes I learned as a teenager.

Perks of Peers and Modesty

The church of our early years was the only one in the county, and it was small. But Mom was in tune with the needs of teenage girls. She wanted us to be acquainted with nearby Christians so we could develop a supportive peer group. Mom always made sure we attended youth rallies, went to Christian summer camp, and participated in activities at Christian colleges. She strongly believed those environments promoted spiritual growth. And she was right. Her ideas worked!

As a testament to our upbringing, morality was woven into our everyday lives. Our sister Donna became our high school's drum majorette. When the band director presented her with the official outfit, Donna promptly asked, "You got anything else?" You see, the skirt was about six inches long from top to bottom! We had been taught well enough to know apparel that scanty was not modest. The director replied, "Well, I have the pants outfit for a boy in that position." Donna chose the pants and went on to lead the band in a glorious way without disappointing God in the process.

CYNTHIA'S TREATS

Some of Judi's teachers encouraged her to enter our "Miss High School" pageant. The contest included a swimsuit competition. Judi knew that parading down a runway in a swimsuit wasn't in keeping with modest Christian behavior. After careful consideration, she decided to enter the competition, but for that particular segment, Judi wore a 1908 swimsuit, complete with pantaloons, puffed sleeves, full skirt, sailor collar, and a parasol. The audience cheered, and Judi walked away with a second-place trophy. Several girls in the pageant admitted they wished they had her courage!

Make a Difference

In our attempt to be popular, we often fail to concern ourselves with favor toward God. What about Mary, the mother of Jesus? She was chosen as one "highly favored and blessed among women" (Luke 1:28–30). Determine to develop yourself toward Christ and stand up for Him even in your first layer of life! That determination will make a difference in the rest of your layers.

How can women in their first twenty years make a stand for Christ in the following areas? Write applicable scriptures.

Dating _____

_____

_____

Ethics (Cheating, etc.) _____

_____

_____

Respect for Authority _____

_____

_____

Political & Moral Issues _____

_____

_____

List two ways to influence teen girls in your congregation to develop themselves spiritually.

1. _____

2. _____

Second Twenty Years

During her second twenty years, a woman's life centers on family—encouraging her husband and raising her children in the nurture and admonition of the Lord. In Titus 2:3–4 Paul urges Timothy to encourage young women to learn from older women how to love their families. This is top priority!

Keep the Home

We women have a God-given role—to be the keeper of the home, a homemaker (Titus 2:5). In today's world, some ladies have a job outside the home, but that should not pre-empt the responsibility of managing the home (1 Timothy 5:14). Some women handle both roles well. Most often, women struggle with balance, and usually the scripturally assigned position suffers.

Put "Eat Chocolate" at the top of your list of things to do today. That way, at least, you'll get one thing done.

We may feel pressured by the world, our bosses, and our peers to be "super-moms"—do it all! But if we are not able to balance management of the home and outside work with good results, we must remember that the top priority is keeping our homes.

Our homes should be places of retreat and rest for our families. Consider these questions:

* Do I keep the home as I should?

* Do my husband and children like to come home?

* Do my husband and children feel free to invite friends and associates to our house?

* Do friends of family members feel welcome when they visit?

Don't let the world's version of the role of women take this joy away from you.

Ask at least five married women with children for their outlook on managing a career and a home. How does it benefit the children when the mother has a career? What reasons does the mother give for choosing to balance two jobs? Report your findings.

_____

_____

_____

Love Husband and Children

Admonish the young women to love their husbands, to love their children, to be discreet, chaste, homemakers, good, obedient to their own husbands, that the word of God may not be blasphemed (Titus 2:4–5).

Why do younger women need to be "taught" to love their husbands? The crux of the matter is, how do we define love? It is not just emotion; it is action! Our generation and the next have been force-fed the idea of taking care of self before anyone else: "Stand up for your rights," and "Don't be taken for granted." But the truth of the following scripture exposes selfishness:

Do nothing from selfishness or empty conceit, but with humility of mind regard one another as more important than yourselves (Philippians 2:3 NASB).

Try this: Read 1 Corinthians 13:4–7 and consider all the attributes of love in action. Read it again putting your name in the place of the word *love*. Are you kind? Are you patient? Do you seek your own? Developing these attributes takes time and practice. Putting these actions into practice is a true way to love your husband as God intended.

> There are four basic food groups: milk chocolate, dark chocolate, white chocolate, and chocolate truffles.

Proverbs 14:1 says, "The wise woman builds her house, but the foolish pulls it down with her hands." Building up one's family through encouraging words and actions takes time and energy. We must have "the law of kindness" on our tongues (Proverbs 31:26) and provide physical care by preparing food, clothing, and "watching over the ways" of our households (Proverbs 31:15, 21, 27). It is not always easy or convenient, but to neglect our loved ones for our own desires and comfort pulls down our houses with our own hands. Many do not realize that until it is too late.

Give your all in training your children. When they are grown, you can find peace in knowing you did your best to bring them up

Older women are like aging strudels—the crust
may not be so lovely, but the filling has come
at last into its own.   —Robert Farrar Capon

properly. If they remain faithful to the Lord, you can rest in the joy
that they walk in truth (3 John 1:4; Proverbs 22:6).

While loving your children, don't forget your husband! Work diligently to maintain a strong bond with him. You don't want to find yourself one day sitting across the table from a stranger. Robert Browning wrote:

> Grow old along with me!
> The best is yet to be,
> The last of life, for which the first was made:
> Our times are in his hand
> Who saith, "A whole I planned,
> Youth shows but half; trust God: see all, nor be afraid.

When God gives us a family, He demands dedication and priority in return. Some say that quality time with your family is all that matters. However, studies show that quantity time is more effective. This middle layer of years is special and unique, for when it is gone, it is gone. There are no do-overs. Godly efforts in the first layer of life will make our second layer—twenty-one to forty years of age—enjoyable and productive.

What did you learn as a child that continues to influence your spiritual walk? As you define the answer below, reflect on how you are passing this trait on to your children. (You may also ask this of another person and share it.)

_____

_____

_____

Third Twenty Years

After the children are grown, a woman has more time to focus on service. When we were younger, we were nurtured by the older women in the church. Some taught us in Sunday school, some prepared the communion each week, some brought food when we were sick. We warmed ourselves with fires built by previous generations.

Paul taught us how to respond in kind. When he was shipwrecked on the island of Malta, he warmed himself with a fire built by others. As time passed, he gathered sticks to fuel the flames (Acts 28:1–3). Church programs wane without help. As older women, we must lay sticks on these fires in our congregations so the younger can be warmed by them.

Seven days without chocolate makes one weak.

Have you heard ladies jokingly say at potlucks that they can't wait to taste that good home cooking by the older women? But if everyone continued to depend on the older ladies to

bring all the good stuff, the future generation's potlucks would consist of the Colonel's crispy original and cookies made by little elves! Older ladies must help those young ones learn such skills so they, in turn, can keep that fire going. And the young women must avail themselves of the sages.

Proverbs 16:31 tells us, "The silver-haired head is a crown of glory, if it is found in the way of righteousness." Let's be proud to be growing older. The longer we live, the longer we can serve.

> So even to old age and gray hairs, O God, do not forsake me, until I proclaim your might to another generation, your power to all those to come (Psalm 71:18 ESV).

> And the things that you have heard from me among many witnesses, commit these to faithful men who will be able to teach others also (2 Timothy 2:2).

How was Caleb an example of strength in his later years? Sarah? Support your answer with scripture.

_____

_____

_____

An Empty Box

When the third layer of a box of chocolates is gone, what is left? An empty box. Someday our lives will end, and we too will end up in empty boxes. Hebrews 9:27 says, "And as it is appointed for men to die once, but after this the judgment." On that day, each of us will answer to God whether her life was like a box of good chocolates or part of a batch that had to be fed to the pigs.

You can tell more about a woman by what people say about her than what she says about others. So what will people say about you when you are gone? Think about it! What kind of life are you living? The lyrics of an old song declare, "Let's give them something to talk about!" Let's make sure that they will talk about our good influences.

In Linda Ellis's poem, "The Dash," she draws attention to the dash between the dates of birth and death on a tombstone. That dash includes the entirety of the life of the deceased. Have someone read "The Dash" aloud. (See www.lindaellis.net.) Write a sentence you would like to be included in your eulogy.

_____

_____

Bible Women and Empty Boxes

Consider Dorcas. When she died the women washed her and laid her in an upper room. Then they sent two men to Joppa to beg Peter to pay them a visit. When Peter arrived, they escorted him to the upper room where all the widows stood weeping, showing the tunics and garments Dorcas had made. Dorcas earned a precious place in the minds

of devout women. We cannot imagine the joy they received when Peter presented her to them alive!

Now think of Jezebel! An idolater, a murderer, a thief, a hater of good, a showgirl! What a big box—empty though it was!

STIRRING SWEETNESS

1. How does the foundation of one layer give strength to the next?

2. Why do you think the God-given role of "keeper at home" is often looked down on in today's society?

3. Why are we never too old to serve God?

WRAPPING IDEAS

Memory makers. Take a box of chocolates to some elderly and shut-ins of the church or community. Let them choose their favorite chocolate. Reminisce with them about some childhood memories the chocolate may bring back. Be sure to leave the box of chocolates when you go!

Focusing on the Inside

SWEET TRUTHS

1 Samuel 16:7

"The Lord does not see as man sees; for man looks at the outward appearance, but the Lord looks at the heart."

Matthew 23:13

"But woe to you, scribes and Pharisees, hypocrites! For you shut up the kingdom of heaven against men; for you neither go in yourselves, nor do you allow those who are entering to go in."

Galatians 6:1

"Brethren, if a man is overtaken in any trespass, you who are spiritual restore such a one in a spirit of gentleness, considering yourself lest you also be tempted."

83

Matthew
6:14–15

"For if you forgive men their trespasses, your heavenly Father will also forgive you. But if you do not forgive men their trespasses, neither will your Father forgive your trespasses."

CENTER

Just as God looks on the heart of each person, so should we.

What's  Inside?

1. Don't judge people by their outward appearance.

2. Don't stereotype.

3. Follow Jesus' example to find those who need help.

4. Forgiveness is a must.

The Heart of the Matter

Most boxes of chocolates are mysterious. The contents boast a variety, but the insides hide under the rich brown covers. Do you have favorites? Cynthia likes texture, lots of nuts and crunch. The more texture, the better. Some of our friends prefer the soft marshmallows and creme.

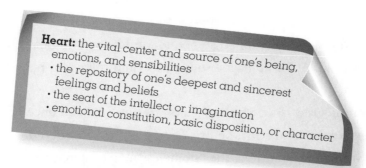

Heart: the vital center and source of one's being, emotions, and sensibilities
• the repository of one's deepest and sincerest feelings and beliefs
• the seat of the intellect or imagination
• emotional constitution, basic disposition, or character

Judi looks for that milk chocolate square with caramel in the center. Her favorite way to ready a chocolate bar for eating is to put it in the microwave for a few seconds. But sometimes she prepares it naturally by putting it on the dash of her car on the way home from the store. By the time she gets home it will be soft, warm, and ready to eat!

Sometimes you can look at the chocolates in the box and guess what's inside them. But you can't always tell—so you pinch one and peek inside.

Life is like that. Around us are people of all sizes, shapes, colors, and personalities. Some invitingly attract enough to make you want to get to know them better. Others? You are more hesitant to meet them. You assume you have nothing in common with them. But just like chocolates, you'll never know what they are like until you peek inside—we don't recommend pinching them. After all, it's what inside that counts!

That's what the Lord says.

The Lord does not see as man sees; for man looks at the outward appearance, but the Lord looks at the heart (1 Samuel 16:7).

> Life without chocolate is like a beach without water.

Homeless Mystery

The story is told of a preacher who decided one Sunday to dress as a homeless man. He went to the church building and sat on the outside

edge of the stoop. He hoped someone would stop and talk to him or invite him in. At least, maybe someone would offer him help. But no one did.

As time grew close for the sermon to start, the audience began to chatter. No one had seen the preacher. Members wondered where he could be. About that time, the "homeless man" entered the building, walked down the aisle, and stepped into the pulpit. He revealed his identity and began his sermon on the danger of a Christian's being a respecter of persons.

Jesus fellowshipped people who were often shunned by others. What unusual people did He choose as friends?

Luke 15:2 _____

Mark 2:16 _____

Luke 7:36–50 _____

Acts 9:8–16 _____

Accepting the Scarred

People today need our unconditional love. Judi's local congregation initiates several outreach ministries: a prison ministry, a divorce recovery program, an addiction recovery program, marriage seminars, and youth programs. So many of society's problems have been overlooked, ignored, and swept under the rug by congregations for too long. The church's "reaching out" needs to be turned into "bringing in." Christians are in the people-loving business.

Is prejudice alive in the church today? God loves everyone and He wants His people to do the same. In Scripture we learn that the Israelites thought they were the only ones God loved. But He called Jonah to preach to Nineveh, and those citizens of that Assyrian capital were the most barbaric people on earth. Jonah did not love them. He wanted them destroyed. But God loved them and wanted them saved. What an example!

> Man created chocolate, and he saw that it was good. Then he separated the light from the dark, and it was better.

Society is becoming a bigger melting pot. The result is an increase in the number of recovering addicts, innocent victims of divorce, and single moms and dads. These hurting people need Christian arms to open wide and fill the void left by tragedy. They need encouragement to overcome the scars. We must imitate Jesus' empathy.

Christians whose tragedies resulted from their own sins need help with feelings of guilt. Our attitude toward them greatly influences their recovery. The New Testament commands us to forgive those who repent. Galatians 6:1 says,

> Brethren, if a man is overtaken in any trespass, you who are spiritual restore such a one in a spirit of gentleness, considering yourself lest you also be tempted.

Scripture also tells us that God's forgiveness of our sins depends on whether or not we forgive others:

For if ye forgive men their trespasses, your heavenly Father will also forgive you: but if ye forgive not men their trespasses, neither will your Father forgive your trespasses (Matthew 6:14–15 KJV).

If an offender truly repents, we have an obligation to forgive him. That means not only accepting him but also doing everything possible to help him in his Christian walk.

How do you and your congregation reach out to repentant sinners?

_____

_____

_____

_____

_____

Galatians 6:9 warns against becoming "weary while doing good." Why is this often the case when we're helping people with "heart" problems?

_____

_____

_____

_____

Denominations

Another prejudice often present among Christians is bias toward those of different faiths. Of course, we are not to embrace false doctrine (2 John 1:10–11), but are we doing enough to reach out to those who have been taught religious error? We don't want others to stereotype us, but are we sometimes guilty of stereotyping others? Jesus pronounced a woe upon those in His day who "shut up the kingdom of heaven against men" (Matthew 23:13).

> Good friends are like fancy chocolates . . . it's what's inside that makes them special.

We must be careful not to decide that others are "unteachable" before we get to know them and their hearts—what's on the inside. People who are already trying to follow God will receive His help in softening their hearts to the truth. Remember the account of Cornelius' conversion (Acts 10).

Write an idea to enable a church to reach out to various ethnic groups and to those of other religious affiliations:

_____

_____

_____

_____

Forgiven

How would the church today treat King David after his repentance of adultery with Bathsheba and the murder of her husband? Would some congregations say he is forgiven and then refuse to allow him to serve? What about us as individuals? Do we say we forgive but then refuse to associate with our penitent brothers and sisters? Does that violate scripture? Are we respecters of persons?

> Vegetables are a must on a diet. I suggest carrot cake, zucchini bread, and pumpkin pie.
>
> —Jim Davis

It has been said that people don't care how much you know until they know how much you care. Jesus fed the hungry; then He taught them. He healed the sick; then He taught them. Reaching out to others and meeting needs present more opportunities to teach the truth, even in difficult situations.

Ask yourself: If everyone reached out to the hurting with the same intensity and as often as I do—even to those who are "different"— would people believe the church cares?

STIRRING SWEETNESS

1. Consider situations in which you misjudged someone and later learned you were wrong.

2. Have you ever been the brunt of prejudice? How did that make you feel?

3. Discuss what true forgiveness involves.

WRAPPING IDEAS

Taste-testing party. Everyone brings her favorite chocolates to share with the group. Then take a poll to determine individual preferences in the group: dark, milk, white, nuts, caramel, and peanut butter. You may find a sister who will become your best friend!

Sister Sue's Velveeta Fudge

1 lb margarine (Yes. I said 1 lb . . . 4 sticks)
1 lb Velveeta cheese
4 lbs powdered sugar (Yes . . . 4 lbs)
1 cup cocoa
1 T vanilla
Nuts (optional)

Melt together margarine and Velveeta over low heat stirring often. (Microwave if you like.) Sift together sugar and cocoa. When mixture is melted, stir in vanilla. Add dry mixture and stir. Keep stirring. (It takes a while but it will become smooth and creamy.)

Add nuts if desired. Spread in a greased 9 x 13 pan. Cool and cut.

Recipe can be divided in half. Or better yet put it in 2 square pans and share some with a friend! Store tightly covered.

Judi says, "If you let people taste it before they know what's in it, they love it. If you tell them it is made with Velveeta cheese, they may not even taste it!"

Lisa's Chocolate Miracle Whip Cake

2 cups flour

1 cup sugar

1½ t baking soda

1½ t baking powder

4 T cocoa

Pinch salt

1 cup Miracle Whip

1 cup water

1 t vanilla extract

Sift the dry ingredients and set aside. Little by little, mix the water into the Miracle Whip to ensure against lumps. Add vanilla. Add the dry ingredients by thirds into the liquids, stirring between until smooth. Pour into a greased, floured 9 x 13 pan and bake at 350 degrees for 30–35 minutes, until the cake begins to pull away from the edge of the pan.

This cake is so moist there is no need for icing, unless you just want more chocolate!

Consulting the Creator

SWEET TRUTHS

Psalm 119:105	"Your word is a lamp to my feet and a light to my path."
2 Timothy 3:16–17	"All Scripture is given by inspiration of God, and is profitable for doctrine, for reproof, for correction, for instruction in righteousness, that the man of God may be complete, thoroughly equipped for every good work."
Proverbs 14:12	"There is a way that seems right to a man, but its end is the way of death."
Jeremiah 10:23	"O Lord, I know the way of man is not in himself; it is not in man who walks to direct his own steps."

| Proverbs 3:6 | "In all your ways acknowledge Him, and He shall direct your paths." |

· ·

| Isaiah 55:8 | "'For My thoughts are not your thoughts, nor are your ways My ways,' says the Lord." |

CENTER

If we follow God's instructions, we will avoid things that will hurt us and will find the things that will help us live a full life.

What's  Inside?

1. God's Word is our instruction sheet.

2. The New Testament is Jesus' will.

3. We don't have to understand everything to follow His will.

Creator Knows Best

How do you feel about the guide sheet that comes with your chocolates? Do you use it to find out what is in each piece? That does enhance the

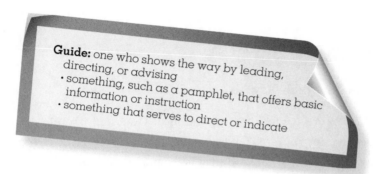

Guide: one who shows the way by leading, directing, or advising
• something, such as a pamphlet, that offers basic information or instruction
• something that serves to direct or indicate

taste, doesn't it? Who prepares the guide sheet and puts it into the box? The creators of the candy, of course! They made the individual pieces, so they know what's inside each.

Have you stopped long enough to realize that the guide sheet is for our benefit? If we disregard that guidance, we could end up biting into things that could hurt us. Some are allergic to nuts or coconut. And what dangers might a diabetic face if she consumes the wrong kind or too much of a particular chocolate? If we follow the guide sheet, we can avoid the harmful while we entertain our palate.

God our Creator knows what is best for us. He gave us a guide sheet made up of sixty-six books. This set of instructions—the Bible— is much more important than the guide sheet in a box of chocolates. Psalm 119:105 tells us that God's instruction manual is a lamp to our feet and a light to our path. Aren't you thankful for that Guide Sheet!

Research the phrase "that it may be well with you" from the scriptures. What is usually the context?

Instruction Manual

What does the Bible have to say for itself?

> All Scripture is given by inspiration of God, and is profitable for doctrine, for reproof, for correction, for instruction in righteousness, that the man of God may be complete, thoroughly equipped for every good work (2 Timothy 3:16–17).

Two very important truths stand out in this Scripture:

1. The Bible is inspired by God.

2. The Bible provides instruction for everything we do in life.

Are you aware that the word *inspiration* in this verse actually means "God breathed"? That helps us view the Scriptures in a whole new light. God didn't merely put scripture into someone's head and have him write it down for us. He "breathed" it—just as He breathed into man the breath of life to make him a living soul (Genesis 2:7). God breathed His instructions to tell us how to make our souls strong and happy. And if we follow them, we will be!

Judi's Sweets

Stan was helping our son Phil put together a swing set for his three kids. They were actually using the instruction sheet. (That is a surprising thing for men to do!) When they started to assemble the last steps, they found that some of the listed parts were missing. Phil called the company and almost immediately the representative said, 'You have model number 101223A, don't you?'

"Yes, that is correct," Phil told her.

She then replied, "You aren't missing any parts. Your box has the wrong instruction sheet. We have changed that particular model and it is put together differently."

Then she emailed him the correct instructions. Everything fit into place!

Many are following the wrong instructions in their attempts to assemble their lives. Some are even trying to assemble life without any instructions at all. In Proverbs 14:12 we find, "There is a way that seems right to a man, but its end is the way of death." Jeremiah 10:23 adds, "The way of man is not in himself; it is not in man who walks to direct his own steps." Find your guide in Proverbs 3:6: "In all your ways acknowledge Him, and He shall direct your paths."

Compare the illustration of the swing set instructions with trying to live life without God's Word.

_____

_____

God's Word explains how to live. He never commands anything that is bad for us, and He never forbids anything that is good for us. If we study and learn His instructions, we can spare ourselves a lot of sorrow.

Purpose in Your Heart

It also pays to have the directions in mind before we begin a task. So many times we consider a project and then proceed without adequate "assembly" knowledge, only to be forced to undo wrongly assembled parts and start over, following the directions.

Judi's Sweets

Stan and I had to disassemble our patio table in preparation for storage. Months later, I tackled the job of reassembling it. *No problem,* I thought. *I know exactly how it's done. After all, I helped to disassemble it.*

So with great confidence, I began to attach the legs to the base—all ten bolts—and tightened each one. Then because of the torque of the legs, I could not attach them under the lip of the table. Ouch!

So I'll have to loosen the bolts, I thought. And I did. That didn't work.

All right. I see the problem. I must remove all the bolts and then attach the legs to the table. Yep! A pretty big redo, but it worked perfectly!

Judi, how about reading the instructions next time? You'll save yourself a lot of grief, because everything in the long run will come out better.

Is there anything in that table-assembly experience that reminds you of life? Yes! We will make mistakes, but if we prepare for life's twists and turns by acquainting ourselves with God's directions, we will avoid many problems along the way. Remember how Daniel "purposed in his heart" not to defile himself with the king's delicacies or with his wine? God's instructions were already in Daniel's heart, so he had no problem making the right decision.

> I was like a chocolate in a box, looking well behaved and perfect in place, all the while harboring a secret center.
>
> —Deb Caletti

Have we been desensitized to the term *testament?* Do you realize that the New Testament is Jesus' will that became effective at His death? He left instructions for humanity that are effective until He comes again. That will is signed in blood and cannot be changed, even though parts of it aren't popular.

Inheriting the Farm

A farmer, knowing his time remaining on earth was short, decided to prepare his will. He left his farm to his son with certain stipulations. The farm would belong to the son if he followed these instructions:

1. Dig a well on the south side of the barn.

2. Plant the corn in the west field.

3. Plant the beans in the far north field.

4. Keep the cattle in the interior pasture.

The son read the will and decided that the south side of the barn was truly the best place for the well. He planted the corn in the west field and the beans in the far north field. But then a problem arose.

Dad was a very intelligent man, he mused. *So I cannot imagine why he wanted me to keep the cattle in the interior pasture. That grass is inferior.*

The other pasture has an abundance of greener and more nutritious grass. I'll put them there.

So he did.

Compare the parable above to Matthew 7:21. Why do you think the son will not inherit the farm?

_____

_____

Some might say, "Well, although the son did not follow all his father's instructions, he changed only one thing."

No, he did not follow his father's will in any of the instructions. He followed only the parts that suited him.

By the way, all the cattle died. The interior pasture was the only area free of poisonous plants. The son did not know that, and he didn't need to know. He needed only to follow his father's instruction. The saying is true: Father knows best.

Too many times we choose to follow God's instructions when they are convenient to us—the ones that don't interfere with our plans.

Chocolate has many preservatives. Preservatives make you look younger.

That is our feeble attempt to bring the Father's will down to our level. God says, "My thoughts are not your thoughts, nor are your ways My ways" (Isaiah 55:8). We should never allow our common sense to supersede our godly sense. Just as in a box of chocolates, the Creator knows best. If we follow God's guide sheet, we can enjoy the best of life and avoid the harmful.

STIRRING SWEETNESS

1. Discuss the binding properties of a will. How does that compare to the New Testament?

2. Why do people want to change God's instructions?

3. Give some examples of things God requires that we might have chosen to do differently.

4. Discuss a decision you made without first seeking God's guidance. Compare that to one you made after seeking His advice.

WRAPPING IDEAS

Prove a point. Before class begins, put an equal number of name-brand and off-brand chocolates into a dish and mix them. Be sure to use enough chocolates so when all students have taken one each, several pieces will be left. Interrupt your lecture briefly to tell the class you are passing chocolates around, and that everyone should choose one to taste. Continue with the lecture while the dish makes its round. When the dish returns, show the class that the remaining chocolates are mostly off-brand.

Here's the point: You know what's in the name brand; you already know it is good. More importantly, you know God's ways are best! Why settle for an off-brand?

Wanda's 3-Minute Chocolate Cake-in-a-Mug

4 T flour

9 T hot chocolate mix

Pinch of salt

1 egg

3 T water

3 T oil

Spray a large microwavable mug with cooking spray. Stir the dry ingredients in the mug. Add egg and stir a bit so the cup doesn't overflow. Stir in water and oil gradually until thoroughly moistened. Make sure to scrape the bottom of the mug to avoid leftover pockets of dry ingredients. Microwave on high for 3 minutes. Tip the cake out of the mug to a dish. Break into quarters for cooling. Eat!

To share: Put all dry ingredients into a clear bag and place inside a decorative mug. Copy this recipe and attach it to the mug with a ribbon. It makes a great gift!

Janie's Southern Brownies

This is a *Southern Living* recipe and the brownies are really good, especially the second day refrigerated.

1 Devils Food cake mix

1 3 oz pkg instant chocolate pudding

2 cups sour cream

1 cup butter

5 large eggs

1 t vanilla

3 cups semisweet morsels

1 cup white chocolate morsels

1 cup chopped pecans, toasted

Mix all ingredients. Pour into a greased 9 x 14 pan and bake at 350 degrees for 30 minutes, or until wooden pick inserted near center comes out clean.

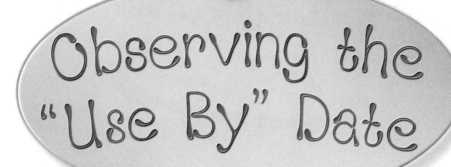

Observing the "Use By" Date

James 4:14

"For what is your life? It is even a vapor that appears for a little time and then vanishes away."

· ·

Matthew 18:3

"Assuredly, I say to you, unless you are converted and become as little children, you will by no means enter the kingdom of heaven."

· ·

John 10:10

"The thief does not come except to steal, and to kill, and to destroy. I have come that they may have life, and that they may have it more abundantly."

CENTER

We, like chocolate, have a limited shelf life, so we need to live life to the fullest.

What's Inside?

1. Life is short.

2. We must wisely use every minute God gives us, for life is a gift.

3. Jesus set an example of finding joy in life.

Don't Wait!

At the Hershey website, one of the most frequently asked questions was, "How long should I keep chocolate?" The answer: "The shelf life of such products is generally a year." So ladies, if you find candy left over from last year's Halloween, eat it before October 31! The website explained, "Products kept beyond recommended shelf life may have flavor loss or texture changes." Whether you like your chocolate crunchy or soft, texture changes are not good. Chocolate is best when it's fresh! We should not put away our box of chocolates, hoping to enjoy it in a few years. The candy will not keep.

Life is the same. There is a tendency to procrastinate instead of enjoying some of the simple things that can bring happiness now. Perhaps you've said, "We'll wait until the children start school, and then we'll . . ." or "We'll wait until we can afford it, then we'll . . ." or "I'll wait until I retire and then I'll . . ."

James 4:14 compares life to a vapor that vanishes. We are not promised tomorrow, so we need to make every day count.

> So teach us to number our days, That we may gain a heart of wisdom.
>
> —Psalm 90:12

There is an untitled, anonymous article appearing on inspirational websites:

Too many people put off something that brings them joy just because they haven't thought about it, don't have it on their schedule, didn't know it was coming, or are too rigid to depart from their routine. I got to thinking one day about all those women on the Titanic who passed up dessert at dinner on that fateful night in an effort to reduce calorie intake. From then on, I've tried to be a little more flexible.

How often have your kids dropped in to talk and sat in silence while you watched "Jeopardy" on television? I cannot count the times I called my sister and said, "How about going to lunch in a half hour?" She would gasp and stammer something like, "I can't. I have clothes on the line"; "My hair is dirty"; "I wish I had known yesterday"; "I had a late breakfast"; or "It looks like rain." And my personal favorite: "It's Monday." She died a few years ago. We never did have lunch together.

If you were going to die soon and could make only one phone call, who would you call and what would you say? And why are you waiting?

—copied

Give your own example of someone who had intentions of doing good and kept procrastinating. Also, give a Bible example.

_____

_____

_____

_____

The Present

Perhaps you've heard this slogan: "Yesterday is history, tomorrow is a mystery, and today is a gift. That's why we call it the present." Every day is a gift from God. He has given it to us to use in His service. Have you stopped to consider that some Christians are praying for loved ones to have another day so they will have another opportunity to obey the gospel? Some are praying for loved ones to live another day in case a cure is found for their disease. This day that you are living right now may be the result of someone else's answered prayer! Maybe someone has been praying for you and today their prayer will be answered. Use each day to the fullest!

When Judi's grandson Drew was small, someone gave him three chocolate kisses during worship. He ate one and put the

> Your hand and your mouth agreed many years ago that, as far as chocolate is concerned, there is no need to involve your brain.
>
> —Dave Barry

other two in his pocket to eat later. Before the end of the sermon, he reached in to get the candy and pulled his hand out, covered with melted chocolate. The heat from his body prevented him from enjoying those pieces. (We mothers are sure thankful for wet wipes, aren't we?) Don't save life for later! Enjoy it now.

Become as Little Children

How do most children eat chocolate? By getting the sweet melted goodness all over their faces, all over their hands, and sometimes, all over their clothes. They enjoy it to the fullest. Well, Matthew 18:3 tells us that except we become as little children, we shall in no wise enter into the kingdom of heaven! Savor life. Laugh. Enjoy.

> Among life's mysteries is how a two-pound box of chocolate can make a person gain five pounds.

The following untitled, anonymous, article should also spur us to live in the moment.

A friend of mine opened his wife's underwear drawer and picked up a package wrapped in silk paper.

"This," he said, "isn't any ordinary package." He unwrapped the box and stared at both the silk paper and the box.

"She got this the first time we went to New York eight or nine years ago. She has never put it on. She was saving it for a special occasion. Well, I guess this is it."

He got near the bed and placed the gift box next to the other clothing he was taking to the funeral home. He turned to me and said: "Never save something for a special occasion. Every day in your life is a special occasion."

I still think those words changed my life. Now I read more and clean less. I sit on the porch without worrying about anything. I spend more time with my family and less at work. I understand that

If you can't eat all your chocolate, it will keep in the freezer. But if you can't eat all your chocolate, what's wrong with you?

life should be a source of experience to be lived up to, not survived through. I no longer save something for special use. I use crystal glasses every day. I'll wear new clothes to go to the supermarket if I feel like it. I don't save my special perfume for special occasions. I use it whenever I want. The words *someday* and *one day* are fading from my dictionary. If it's worth seeing, hearing, or doing, I want to see it, listen to it, or do it—now!

I don't know what my friend's wife would have done if she had known she wouldn't be there the next morning. This nobody can tell. I think she might have called her relatives and closest friends.

She might have called old friends to make peace over past quarrels. I'd like to think she would have gone out for Chinese, her favorite food. It's these small things that I would regret not doing if I knew my time had come. I would regret it, because I would no longer see the friends I would meet, letters . . . letters that I wanted to write "one of these days." I would regret and feel sad, because I didn't tell my brothers and sons, not enough times at least, how much I loved them.

Now I try not to delay, postpone, or keep anything that could bring laughter and joy into our lives. And each morning I say to myself that this could be a special day. Each day, each hour, each minute is special.

—Selected

Postpone: to put off or delay until a future time; to put behind in order of importance

Are you one of those people who saves her good china for company? If so, get it out and use it with your loved ones. Sister Counts used to say, "Do your giving while you're living, so you'll be knowing where it's going." God has blessed us with so many things in this life, but they are all meant to be used! Not only used but used in His service!

Flowers and sweet words may set the stage, but it's chocolate that steals the show.

Consider how God blessed Solomon: land, riches, possessions—but above all, wisdom. How did he use his wisdom to glorify God? In later years, he failed in his mission to serve God. What was the cause of his failure? How can we use our blessings to glorify God?

Jesus Lived the Abundant Life

Scripture reveals only a few years of Jesus' earthly life, but it tells how He lived it. He knew how to put first things first, yet he took time for little children. He taught constantly, yet he always took time to rest and pray. He developed close friendships—Peter, James, and John. He went to weddings and funerals. He enjoyed eating with folks—even publicans! We sometimes fail to stop and think of Jesus as flesh and blood. He left the luxuries of heaven but still found happiness here. He said in John 10:10, "I have come that they might have life, and that they may have it more abundantly." Surely we can follow His example.

In order to enjoy life to the fullest, we must do the things we have been putting off. We must slow down, relax, smell the roses, hug our children, eat more chocolate, and be still and know that God is.

 ## STIRRING SWEETNESS

1. Why do we sometimes feel guilty for enjoying our pleasures and treasures?

2. Discuss the things you remember most about your childhood and note that they aren't things at all.

3. Make a list of items in your home that you haven't used in five years. How might each be used to give joy today?

4. List two enjoyable activities that you have been putting off, and do them this week.

5. Compare the emotional ups and downs Jesus experienced on earth to our own ups and downs. How was He still able to live life to the fullest?

WRAPPING IDEAS

Chocolate swap. Have everyone in the group make four dozen pieces of her favorite chocolate cookie or candy. Put one dozen on the tasting table; put the other three dozen on the swapping table. Everyone gets to taste everything, and then take home three dozen pieces of everyone else's chocolate creations.

Easy 1-Minute Chocolate Oatmeal Cookies

2 cups sugar
½ cup cocoa
½ cup milk
1 stick butter or margarine
2 cups quick oats
½ cup peanut butter
½ cup coconut or chopped nuts
1 t vanilla

Mix sugar, cocoa, milk, and butter in a saucepan and boil one minute. Add peanut butter, coconut (and/or nuts), vanilla, and oats. Drop by spoonfuls on waxed paper or buttered cookie sheet.

Cindy says, "I use ¼ recipe when I want a quick candy bar size treat."

Velma's Chocolate Pudding or Pie

¾ cup of sugar

2 T cocoa (or to taste)

2 ½ T corn starch

2 cups milk

3 large eggs

1 t vanilla

3 T butter/margarine

Mix sugar, cocoa, corn starch.

Add enough milk to make a paste.

Add eggs.

Add balance of milk, vanilla, and butter.

Cook until thick.

Pour into pudding cups or a pre-baked pie shell.

Let cool and serve.

Anticipating the Taste

SWEET TRUTHS

Romans 5:1–4

"Therefore, having been justified by faith, we have peace with God through our Lord Jesus Christ, through whom also we have access by faith into this grace in which we stand, and rejoice in hope of the glory of God. And not only that, but we also glory in tribulations, knowing that tribulation produces perseverance; and perseverance, character; and character, hope."

James 1:2–4

"My brethren, count it all joy when you fall into various trials, knowing that the testing of your faith produces patience. But let patience have its perfect work, that you may be perfect and complete, lacking nothing."

Romans 8:28

"And we know that all things work together for good to those who love God, to those who are the called according to His purpose."

CENTER

Life often gives us things we didn't expect. With God, we can handle whatever we are given.

What's  Inside?

1. Life hands us good and bad circumstances.

2. How we handle these makes all the difference.

3. Some situations require more strength to get through.

4. We must be patient and let God work in our lives.

Surprise!

Have you ever selected a piece of candy from a box of chocolates, thinking it was one of your favorites like soft caramel or peanut butter, but it turned out to be one you didn't like?

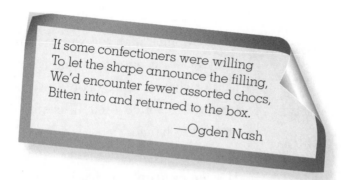

If some confectioners were willing
To let the shape announce the filling,
We'd encounter fewer assorted chocs,
Bitten into and returned to the box.

—Ogden Nash

Here's one chocolate you wouldn't want to eat! In World War II the German army developed a special, lethal candy. This ordinary-looking chocolate bar was really a hand grenade. It was made of steel with a thin covering of real chocolate. When the end of the bar was broken, it stretched a canvas strip which, after seven seconds, caused a deadly explosion.

Sometimes life is like that. We reach for something we think is good, but when we start to use it, it blows up in our faces. God never promised us only what we want in life. We are going to face a few things we didn't choose. How we handle these makes all the difference.

Here is how one woman handled a difficult situation:

Jennifer's wedding day was fast approaching. Her mother had found the perfect dress to wear, but a week later, Jennifer learned that her father's new young wife had bought an identical dress. Jennifer asked the new wife to exchange it, but she stubbornly refused. Jennifer's mother kindly offered to buy herself a different dress. She did.

After shopping, Jennifer asked her mother, "Aren't you going to return the other dress? You really don't have another occasion to wear it."

Her mother sweetly replied, "Of course I do, dear. I'm wearing it to the rehearsal dinner the night before the wedding!"

> Eat a square meal a day—a box of chocolate.

Some days you get the candy bar, some days you get the wrapper.

We women want to fix everything, but in the real world not everything is fixable. We cannot change other people. We must pray for God to soften their hearts so they will make the change.

Neither can we change all situations. How many people are battling terminal cancer, grieving over a lost loved one, or dealing with a failed marriage or prodigal children? Some are trapped in a job they hate. Some struggle with daily pressures of raising children or caring for elderly parents. The Serenity Prayer offers helpful advice:

God grant me the serenity
To accept the things I cannot change,
Courage to change the things I can,
And wisdom to know the difference.

Why does our human side want to retaliate or become bitter when we are handed difficult situations? Discuss "what would Jesus do?" using a Bible example.

Our Model

How should we handle the distasteful "chocolates" we are forced to swallow—the difficult situations we cannot change?

> Chocolate is cheaper than therapy and you don't need an appointment.
>
> —Anonymous

Jesus provided a model in His Gethsemane experience. He was facing a cup He didn't want to drink—death on the cross as sin-bearer for the world. He prayed, "If it is possible, let this cup pass from Me" (Matthew 26:39). It's all right to pray for deliverance from our difficulties. But note Jesus' attitude, "Nevertheless, not as I will, but as You will." He trusted God. Without His death on the cross, we would have no hope of heaven. The Father knows best.

Strength for Troubled Times

The Father also provides strength to handle what we cannot change. As Jesus prayed, "an angel appeared to Him from heaven, strengthening Him" (Luke 22:43). We can ask God to help us change what we can change and to give us the strength to handle what we cannot.

List two ways God has provided strength in your trials.

_____

_____

_____

_____

Sometimes we anticipate a tragedy, but then we are pleasantly surprised when the situation is reversed. How was this the case in 2 Kings 7:3–8?

_____

_____

_____

Expect the Unexpected

James tells us how to deal with the difficult situations God allows us to go through.

> Consider it all joy, my brethren, when you encounter various trials, knowing that the testing of your faith produces endurance. And let endurance have its perfect result, so that you may be perfect and complete, lacking in nothing (James 1:2–4 NASB).

Here, have some chocolate. Feel better now?

Judi's daughter, who has a personal training license, has put her through an exercise program that taught Judi an age-old lesson: strength does not come without pain! But she also learned that exercise becomes easier as you continue to work through it. If you give up, you have to start all over and go through the rough pain again. That principle applies to life. Whatever life hands you, you can gain strength by working through it!

The following article illustrates that point. It was found in a church bulletin.

The Emperor Moth

A man found an emperor moth cocoon. He decided to take it home so he could watch the moth emerge. After waiting patiently for several days, a small opening appeared in the cocoon. The man sat and watched for several hours as the moth struggled to force its body through the little hole. Finally, the moth seemed to stop making progress; it had apparently given up. Out of kindness, the man decided to lend a hand. With a pair of scissors, he snipped off the remaining bit of the cocoon so the moth could get out. The moth soon emerged with a swollen body and small shriveled wings. The man fully expected the body to shrink and the wings to grow strong enough to support the moth in flight. Neither happened.

The bloated moth spent the rest of its life crawling around on the floor. The kind man did not understand that the restricting cocoon and the struggle required for the moth to emerge were necessary to move fluids from the moth's body to its wings. Without the struggle, there could be no flight.

—Selected

> Part of the secret of a success in life is to eat what you like and let the food fight it out inside.
>
> —Mark Twain

Sometimes people ask, "Why does God allow—even demand—trials and tribulations to come on those He loves?" Because we derive great benefit from the struggle. Each trial we face teaches us more about ourselves. We don't see things as God sees them. As the song says, "He's still working on me, to make me what I ought to be."

What difficulties are you going through right now? How might God be working on you? Write a Bible verse here that will give you strength.

_____

_____

Our Purifier

Sometimes we have to be put through the fire to be purified. Malachi 3:3 tells us that God sits "as a refiner and a purifier of silver." What does that mean?

The silversmith says he must hold the silver and keep his eyes on it while it is in the fire. If it is left in the flames a minute too long, it will be destroyed.

How does he know when the silver is fully refined? "Oh, that's easy," he says, "when I see my image in it."

> He will sit as a refiner and a purifier of silver; He will purify the sons of Levi, and purge them as gold and silver, that they may offer to the Lord an offering in righteousness (Malachi 3:3).

What was the purpose of the purification process?

_____

_____

Prayer and Fasting

God is looking to see His reflection in us. We will have to go through some trials so we will look to Him. We find help in Philippians 4:13: "I can do all things through Christ who strengthens me." God also gives us His Spirit to strengthen the inner man (Ephesians 3:16). This helps us to "count it all joy" when we go through tough times. They are opportunities to gain strength!

Judis Sweets

In a recent sermon, my husband, Stan, brought out the following thought that really hit home. In Matthew 17:14–21, Jesus' disciples were unable to heal a demon-possessed man. After Jesus pointed out that their faith was lacking, He said, "However, this kind does not go out except by prayer and fasting!" Stan observed, "Maybe Jesus was telling us that some problems are bigger than others and require more of us!"

When "what we get" seems too much for us to handle, we pray. But fasting is also mentioned numerous times in the Word of God. In the Sermon on the Mount, Jesus said "when you fast," implying that there would be occasions to fast.

Fasting is usually linked with prayer. The intended purpose is two-fold. You are sacrificing something personal (your food) and you get a

constant reminder (hunger pangs) to remind you to pray. If you have never tried fasting in the face of extreme difficulty, give it a try. It could be that your problem is one that "only comes out with prayer and fasting"!

Where's the Gratitude?

Hey! Enough about the piece of chocolate you didn't like! What about the ones you love! So many times in our lives God blesses us with great things. Not only are they the things He knows are good for us, but they are things we enjoy as well. As Christians, we must never forget to be thankful for the good things in life. Remember what Noah did as soon as he exited the ark? He built an altar and thanked God for saving him and his family. How often do we receive great things but forget to thank God! It may be a prayer that was answered in a way we had hoped. It may be that someone you love has turned his or her life around. It may be as simple as waking up without that awful headache you have struggled with for several days.

> My mother's menu consisted of two choices: "Take it or leave it."
>
> —Buddy Hackett

We can use the good things as a springboard for spreading the gospel. The next time your neighbor tells you some good news, say, "Isn't God good to us!" Let's not take God's goodness for granted! If we remember to give Him the praise and glory, He just might see fit to let our next piece of chocolate be something we absolutely love!

Weaving Our Tapestries

Life is sometimes compared to a tapestry. From underneath, it can look like a jumbled mess of dark and light threads and knots. But without the contrast of dark and light, the pattern on top would not be so beautiful. God is embroidering your life and, though at times we can see only the under side, He is in control of the pattern on top. One day when He gets finished with the embroidery, we will get to see the whole picture!

Compare Ephesians 2:10 with Romans 9:20–23, keeping in mind that we are God's handiwork—His tapestry. How can we prevent our tendency to grumble about our "tapestry"?

_____

_____

It's Up to You

Life is like a box of chocolates: dark chocolate, light chocolate, milk chocolate, caramel, coconut, covered nuts. Whatever your box of chocolates offers, whatever life hands you at any given time, it can be a changing point in your life. How you handle it is up to you. We pray that your Christian walk may be filled with more delicious moments because of *Sweet Truths*.

 STIRRING SWEETNESS

1. Discuss this idea: "We can't always fix everything."

2. How can changing what we pray for make things better?

3. What situations do you think would warrant fasting? Why?

4. Think about the good things that have happened in your life just this week. Every good and perfect gift comes down from the Father of lights (James 1:17). Did you think to pray?

 WRAPPING IDEAS

1. *Ladies' Day.* Place a huge box of chocolates at the registration table. Give each attendee a piece and ask her to eat it later. No one gets to choose. Just before the lesson, ask each to bite into her candy. It is interesting to watch. Some will be very happy with what they receive. Others will grimace in disgust, for they must swallow what they don't like. What a great lead-in illustration to the event's theme: "Life is like a box of chocolates. You never know what you're going to get."

2. *Fellowship.* Get together with a group of friends and bring different kinds of chocolate. Divide the pieces into plain bags, one kind in each bag. As a group, with eyes closed, taste the chocolate from one bag. Write down your impression of what you tasted: texture, taste, good or bad, like or dislike. Do the same for each bag. Then compare notes. It is amazing how the same chocolate can be the best for some and the worst for others!

RECIPE INDEX

Notes